A CAMERA IN THE HILLS

*This book is dedicated to the
memory of WAP's only son,*
JOHN BERNARD POUCHER *(1920–2007),*
*who died during the preparation of this book,
and who contributed massively to it.*

A CAMERA IN THE HILLS

THE LIFE AND WORK OF W.A. POUCHER

ROLY SMITH

F

FRANCES LINCOLN LIMITED
PUBLISHERS

Frances Lincoln Ltd
4 Torriano Mews
Torriano Avenue
London NW5 2RZ
www.franceslincoln.com

A Camera in the Hills
Copyright © Frances Lincoln 2008
Text copyright © Roly Smith 2008
Photographs copyright © The Estate of W.A. Poucher

First Frances Lincoln edition: 2008

A catalogue record for this book is available from the British Library.

ISBN 13: 978-0-7112-2898-6

Printed and bound in China

9 8 7 6 5 4 3 2 1

CONTENTS

FOREWORD:
A PHOTOGRAPHIC WAINWRIGHT

There can be few hill walkers of a certain age whose bookcases do not contain one or more books by Walter Poucher. For over two decades after the Second World War his name was synonymous with mountain photography, while his prolific pictorial books inspired several generations to take to the hills, pointing them in the right direction when they got there.

In this I would compare him to Alfred Wainwright. Both had a profound influence on the hill walking game, both doing a similar task in their own idiosyncratic way and both held in great affection by many aficionados – although scorned by others.

As one might expect from a photographer at his prime fifty years ago, Poucher's work is dated. Compared to the modern images of, say, a Colin Monteath or a Gordon Stainforth, his pictures are primitive. While his cherished 35mm Leica (rangefinder) cameras fitted his Jaguar-quality reputation and were, in their portability, a breakthrough from the larger cameras typically used by landscape photographers until the 1960s, they certainly cramped his style with their very limited choice of lenses. Quality Japanese SLRs were revolutionising professional photography by 1960.

Monochrome photography, essentially a translation of what one sees, seems to have been much more Poucher's forte than his colour work. Indeed, many of the colour images in his later, purely pictorial, books seem to be mere snaps, occasionally even banal. The black-and-white pictures in the smaller guidebook-type volumes are much more selective and atmospheric and, where the white route line is superimposed, truly useful.

Though to my mind he was no artist, adding little personal interpretation to his images, Walter Poucher was a technician, a faithful recorder of what he saw, doing it with selective expertise and enthusiasm. His wide coverage of ground in so doing must be the envy of all who love our British hills.

John Cleare, Fonthill Gifford, 2008

1. INTRODUCTION: THIS WAY UP

I first became aware of W.A. Poucher as I toiled up the interminable, lung-bursting treadmill of Brown Tongue on my first ascent of England's highest mountain, Scafell Pike, some time in the mid-1960s.

My only previous visit had been a few years before, during an abortive attempt as part of an ill-equipped secondary modern school party coming from the flatlands of East Anglia. When the geography teacher advised us that, in addition to the sheet sleeping bag needed for the apparently vermin-ridden youth hostel bunks, we would also need boots and water-proofs, most of us innocently opted for the then-fashionable elastic-sided Chelsea boots and a black plastic mac. That day a few years later my hill-walking equipment hadn't improved very much. But a love of walking to high places had been firmly implanted by such school trips, for which I'll always be grateful.

My winkle pickers had already given me a fair amount of grief on the rough, stony path as I had contoured round the broad, grassy shoulder of Lingmell from Wasdale Head and then up the seemingly endless slog of Brown Tongue. I was soon to find out that it would be magnified a thousand times when I began the tortuous descent back down to Wasdale. Thank God I didn't need the mac.

I'd collapsed in an untidy, sweaty and blistered heap on a convenient pathside stone in the great basin beneath Pike's Crag at Hollowstones, and was admiring the impressive rock architecture of Scafell Crag opposite, split by the deep gash of Deep Ghyll and Lord's Rake. Born and brought up on the flint and chalk uplands of north-west Essex, I'd never seen so much naked rock in my life before. Suddenly I noticed an immaculately equipped

OPPOSITE: Walter Poucher, a rising young star in the world of perfumery.

Brown Tongue and Scafell, from *The Lakeland Peaks*.

walker steam into view up the path, clad in a crisp Ventile anorak, Bukta rucksack and shining waxed walking boots, and looking as fresh as a daisy.

'Which route are you taking then?' he asked brightly as he approached.

'I dunno mate,' I gasped, 'The quickest one to the top I expect.'

'Well,' sighed this vision of mountaineering perfection, pulling a neat little pocket-sized guidebook from his rucksack, 'Poucher recommends bearing left here to avoid the *mauvais pas* at Mickledore.' And he pointed to a black-and-white photograph of the scene in the book, with a spidery white line etched across it, clearly showing the route ahead.

Wondering who the hell this 'Poucher' was, and what on earth was a *mauvais pas*, I just caught a glimpse of the title of the book, *The Lakeland Peaks*, and the photograph of Great Gable on the cover, as the experienced fellwalker scornfully strode off towards the Lingmell col, leaving me spluttering in his wake. Next day, recovered from my ultimately successful if rather amateurish climb, I spent the princely sum (for me then) of 25s (£1.25) on *The Lakeland Peaks*, in a Grasmere bookshop.

Thereafter, and for most of my early years of hillwalking, Poucher's masterful pocket-sized 'Pictorial guides to walking . . . and the safe ascent of . . . principal mountain groups' guided me, as they did thousands of others, to most of the summits of the Lakeland, Pennine, Welsh and Scottish peaks. The great advantage was, of course, that Poucher's unique method of inscribing the route across his beautiful black-and-white studies of each mountain meant that a beginner like me didn't need to know how to read a map – which at the time, I certainly didn't.

It was only later that I learned how to map read and enjoy plotting my own routes up the hills, and later still that I discovered Walter Poucher's undoubted genius as the doyen of post-War British mountain photographers. I avidly collected his earlier photographic books, the Chapman & Hall volumes beautifully printed in the soft sepia of photogravure and the Country Life books in the smooth graduated greys of half-tones. They were ideal companions on the days when I was stranded in the lowlands, far from the beckoning hills. In my own mind, I was sure that was one of the main reasons Poucher had produced them too, because I was always fascinated by the exclusive-sounding, stockbroker belt address with which he signed the prefaces to those walking guides: Heathfield, Reigate Heath, Surrey.

Then there was also his shining Jaguar car, which often found its way into the foreground of roadside shots; his crumpled Bukta rucksack topped by a bobble hat, which sometimes served the same purpose up in the hills; and the iconic portrait of the great man himself on the back cover wearing that bobble cap, tweed golfing plus-twos and with his hand on his trusty Leica slung around his neck. His steely eyes were set on the distant horizon, as if searching out the best route to the next summit – or maybe he was just waiting for the clouds to come right.

The introductions to the books not only told you which were the best centres to stay at to explore each range of hills, but what equipment you should be wearing (including a different type of boot in each volume); which were the best viewpoints and best times of the day for photography, and an explanation of the mysterious 'Golden Section' – 'as favoured by great artists such as El Greco, Leonardo, Raphael and Tintoretto' – in photographic compositions.

His flowery literary style always fascinated me too; it was like a throwback from a distant generation, much of which had been lost in the carnage of the First World War. A hill could never be just a hill to Poucher – it became a 'lofty eminence' covered in 'fantastic pinnacles' which, in winter, might be covered not in white but wearing 'a snowy raiment'. A well wooded area was never just that, it was always described as 'sylvan', the photographer was a 'camera artist' and his photographs were often not just pictures but 'camera studies'. Similarly, a viewpoint became a 'coign of vantage' or a 'belvedere'. As a journalist, I knew the style was antiquated and over the top, but I loved it just the same.

One reviewer actually praised Poucher for his revival of the word 'belvedere', which comes from the Italian *bel vedere* and literally means 'beautiful sight'. No less a literary authority than the distiguished critic Ivor Brown paid tribute to Poucher's use of the word in his *I Give You My Word* published in 1948.

'I was happy to find this formal, Italianate term in Mr W.A. Poucher's *Escape to the Hills*,' wrote Brown. 'Mr Poucher is an expert photographer, and he must be a man of infinite patience as well of rare agility in order to obtain his clear, cloudless [*sic*] views of our so often sodden and bemisted peaks. Belvedere is a favourite word of his for the right niche to stop at in order to look, and to wonder. His use of belvedere is certainly justified by the pictures he collects.' Brown added that he had recently confirmed Poucher's opinion of Hall's Fell Top on Blencathra as 'an admirable belvedere' on a recent personal expedition in the Lakes.

As an example of Poucher's typically full-blooded and unrestrained style, this is his description of the extensive panorama from Hall's Fell Top in his *Escape to the Hills* (1943):

> I have sat here by the cairn on several occasions in both summer and winter, but the snow-clad prospect always appeals to me as infinitely

more beautiful. To the south-east you look along the full length of the High Street Range, where Ill Bell appears as a white cone at its southern extremity. The Helvellyn Range is seen end-on, and as such is not impressive, but this is compensated for by the charming vista on the right which carries the eye over the Vale of St John to rest finally upon the tree-girt waters of Thirlmere. The fells immediately to the west of the lake are too high to permit of a sight of the Langdales, but the Central Fells rise majestically above them on the horizon. Further to the south-west the scene is magnificent. Here you look down upon the gleaming surface of Derwentwater, above which all the familiar peaks from Gable to Grisedale Pike rise into the background. The high ridges between them, crowned here and there by a well-known eminence, fade away one after the other into the dim distance beyond.

To the west, the ridge on which you are standing bends slightly to the left to Gategill Fell, while farther away Skiddaw presents a completely changed appearance, its sprawling bulk descending to the right towards the vast solitudes of Skiddaw Forest. The walk along this airy ridge is delightful, and when you begin the descent to Keswick the western panorama is spread out at your feet almost until you reach the foot of the mountain.

And with a nod to his love of skiing and his appreciation of the opportunities presented there, he added: 'This tremendous slope is a splendid ski-ing ground when snow conditions are good, because it is well covered with grass and thus free from danger.'

Poucher described the route up the splendid, narrow rock arete of Hall's Fell Top which, unusually for the Lakes, leads directly to the 868m/2,847ft summit, a little more prosaically in his *Climbing with a Camera: The Lake District* (1963):

However, those of any age who are used to heights would seldom falter here and, moreover, this route culminates in the reward of surprise; for on attaining Hall's Fell Top the ground falls away at one's feet as if by magic and the whole of northern Lakeland is laid bare almost as though one were looking at an aerial map of the district.

Poucher was to take one of his most memorable photographs, which first appeared in *Climbing with a Camera* and later in *The Lakeland Peaks*, of the receding ridges of Hall's Fell, Doddick Fell and Blencathra summit from nearby Scales Fell one snowy winter's afternoon. The low light of the declining winter sun imparts a marvellous velvety texture to the snow on the glorious perspective of the receding ridges, and Poucher's own figure on the extreme right of the photograph, wearing his trademark bobble-hat and golfing plus-twos, gives the whole composition a pleasing human scale.

He described the 'photo opportunity' presented by this scene in *Climbing with a Camera*:

> The quickest and easiest descent is by the broad eastern spur of Scales Fell, and this is the most rewarding for photographers because the afternoon light illuminates the crests of the spurs which stand out clearly above their shadowed flanks. In fact, in good snow conditions such a picture might well be mistaken for the glistening aretes of some Alpine giant.

* * *

Poucher's position as one of the most popular and certainly the most prolific British mountain photographers during the immediate post-War years until perhaps the 1970s was unsurpassed. He was recognised as being the doyen of the art, which until then had been the preserve of climbers such as Frank Smythe, Gerald Lacey and Robert Adam, or Ansel Adams, the master portrayer of California's Sierra Nevada (John Muir's 'Range of Light') and in particular, the soaring granite walls of Yosemite.

Climbing with a Camera: Poucher surveys the icy spurs of Blencathra

During those years, whenever a mountain photograph was required, Poucher unfailingly seemed to be the man who was asked to provide it. His work appeared in numerous books, such as the many countryside titles published by Odhams Press, in national or regional newspapers or the *Radio Times*, in his regular multiple page pictorial features for *Country Life* and *Scottish Life*, or in the new breed of climbing and walking magazines that had just started to appear, such as *Mountain Life, Mountain Craft, Mountain* or *Climber and Rambler* (later *The Great Outdoors* and in its current manifestation, *TGO*).

But Poucher the mountain photographer was only one of his many different personas. After his life-changing service with the Royal Army Medical Corps as a quartermaster dispenser and later captain during the First World War, which included three horrific years on the Western Front, Poucher came back to 'Blighty' determined to make his mark as a cosmetic chemist.

He soon became very well known and respected in his own professional circles as 'the Father of British Perfumery,' and was employed for more than thirty years as the chief perfumer at Yardley, the biggest cosmetics company in Britain and one of the largest in the world at the time. His first book was the standard, three-volume work on perfumes, *Perfumes, Cosmetics and Soaps*, published by Chapman & Hall in 1923. It is still in print and recognised as the bible on the subject. He was also credited with the creation of some of Yardley's most famous perfumes, such as its popular and best-selling Bond Street and Freesia ranges. Such was his international standing in the world of perfumery that Poucher was honoured both in Britain and in America for his pioneering work.

His financial success as a perfumer and the author of the best-selling standard work on the subject gave him the security of needing to work for only six months of the year, so the other six months could be spent in the mountains on his abiding passion of mountain photography. Poucher often stayed in top hotels in the hills and at times waited for weeks for the right conditions to capture a certain image and the illusive mountain light. He once explained to a journalist who had asked him for the secret of his success: 'No one else has the time, dear boy, nor the talent.'

And of course, Poucher was well known in mountaineering circles for the fact that not only did he invent and produce the cosmetics, he actually wore many of them himself. There are many apocryphal tales of walkers who met this vision

Poucher's big question mark. A strange cloud formation (probably a vapour trail shaped by the wind) which Poucher photographed over the Lairig Ghru in 1965, and which was used on the cover of Affleck Gray's *The Big Grey Man of Ben MacDhui* in 1970.

of loveliness on the hill – an immaculately turned out hillwalker complete with mascara, blusher, eye-shadow and lipstick. His profession apparently caused amusement in some climbing circles, among whom he was described as 'a perfume salesman who wears his wares'.

His son John said he thought that his father was testing the cosmetics out on himself, but Poucher always said that it was the responsibility of every man to make the most of himself – and that certainly didn't make him what he termed a 'pansy'. Indeed, Poucher always had a eye for the ladies, and his professional mission in life was to make them more beautiful through cosmetics. And they seemed to like him, too. A secret female admirer once sent him eight red roses while he was staying at the Loch Torridon Hotel, but to his lasting chagrin, he never found out who she was.

And no less an authority on make-up, the Hollywood superstar Elizabeth Taylor once complimented Poucher on his appearance when they met briefly at a Swiss ski resort, and told him that he was one of the best look-ing men she'd ever met in her life. Many women journalists, such as Sue Arnold and Janet Street-Porter, also fell under his undoubted charms.

Poucher's promotion of male cosmetics, including scent and deodorant, was actually far ahead of its time. Nowadays, of course, most men wear some sort of cosmetics, whether it is skin toner, after-shave or deodor-ants, but in Poucher's time, he was often seen as something of an eccentric or even a freak. Men just didn't wear that kind of thing then, and he must have attracted some quizzical looks, especially when he rolled up in his Alvis Grey Lady or Jaguar car at a youth hostel in the heart of the hills. But Poucher had foretold the future for men's cosmet-ics as early as the 1930s.

Born in the final years of the nineteenth century, the son of a Lincolnshire corn merchant, this amazing character could also have had yet another career – as a concert pianist. As a youngster, he was a very accom-plished player and became something of a child prodigy, giving several sell-out concerts in his native Horncastle, but he was finally dissuaded from this career by his father, who told him that he could well end up as a church organist giving lessons to children in some anonymous small country town. That would not have been good enough for Poucher, who, according to his son John, had to excel in everything he did.

It is unfortunate that the only memory most people other than those in the outdoors world will have of Poucher was of his one and only appearance on national television, in a scene which was voted third in an all-time list of 'Top TV Tantrums'. His 1981 appearance, arranged by Constable's Miles Huddlestone, on the live ITV Russell Harty chat show alongside the late Lord Patrick Lichfield will always be remembered for the outrageous attack by the fiery singer and actress Grace Jones on Harty. The show's rather camp host, who had seemed to be slightly unnerved by Poucher's obvious use of make-up (applied for the occasion by his former colleague, Christina Stuart, Yardley's cosmetic chemist), had turned his back on Jones to ask a question of his other guests. As Jones flailed her arms aggressively at Harty, accusing him of ignoring her, Poucher looked on in the background, utterly amazed. Eventually, his usual *sang froid* in disarray, he turned his head towards the equally astonished Patrick Lichfield and a wry smile crossed his lips.

This undeserved claim to fame came towards the end of Poucher's long life. He lived to the age of ninety-six, dying in 1988 in the Thornthwaite nursing home where he spent the last years of his life overlooking Bassenthwaite and his beloved Skiddaw and the northern fells of Lakeland.

Many tributes were paid to Poucher in obituaries in most of the national newspapers and outdoor press. A former perfumer colleague at Yardley, Robert Calkin, summed up the man: 'To the end of his life, he maintained a supreme confidence in his own worth and ability. But this never came across as conceit, and he always maintained an old world courtesy in his relation to others. Few people could have covered so wide a range of creative work with such success.'

But perhaps the finest tribute came from his son John, who was also involved in the perfume business and looked after his father's photographic archives. 'He was an ambitious man whose desire was to excel in whatever he undertook,' said John. 'He died full of years after a marvellous life with,

I would imagine, most of his ambitions fulfilled.' When you think about it, that's not a bad way to end up.

In this illustrated biography, I have used many of Poucher's best photographs to tell the story of that marvellous life – a life in which he seemed to win honours and plaudits in whatever he did. He made the life of his biographer much easier by keeping almost everything he wrote and published, or what was written about him, in a series of scrapbooks which date back to the 1940s and were kept by his son and grandson.

I have also spoken to many of the dwindling band of people who actually knew or worked with him to get their impressions of the great man. In this quest, I was tirelessly assisted by his late son John Poucher, who from the outset lent his unstinting support to the project.

2. EARLY YEARS AND FAMILY AFFAIRS

The sleepy little market town of Horncastle lies at the south-western tip of the rolling Lincolnshire Wolds on the site of the Roman station of Banovallum, whose foundations lie on the tongue of land between the River Waring and the River Bain, from which it took its name.

It is one of the principal market towns serving this predominately agricultural area, but the modern street markets in the leafy market place are nowhere near the scale of the enormous ten-day horse fairs for which Horncastle was once famous. These massive events were held annually here up until the nineteenth century, when buyers from all over the country descended on Horncastle to buy and sell their working horses.

There are a number of pleasant brick houses and some fine old inns in the town, notably The Fighting Cocks, which still has the cock-pit in the yard where this now-illegal sport was practised. Equally bloodthirsty were the bull-baiting sessions staged in the eponymous Bull Ring as late as 1835.

Other mid-nineteenth-century buildings which Walter Poucher would have known in his youth include the grocer's shop which was started by Henry Lunn, who later became famous as a travel agent, founding the internationally known travel company Lunn's Tours.

The parish church of St Mary near the Market Place has a massive, low tower with a little 'candle-snuffer' beacon. There are many Civil War relics in the church, including pikes and scythes, from the Battle of Snipe Dales, which took place on 11 October 1643 just to the east of Horncastle, and which for historians is probably Horncastle's main claim to fame.

* * *

Poucher's maternal family, photographed by Carltons in 1890. It shows (left to right): Charles Dixon (grandfather), Clara Poucher (sister), Arthur Dixon (uncle), Rachel Poucher (mother), John Poucher (father), WAP (aged four) and Esther Dixon (grandmother).

William Arthur Poucher was born in a brick terraced house at 22 Queen Street, Horncastle on 22 November 1891, the first child of John and Rachel Poucher, *née* Dixon. The couple later had another son, Charles Herbert, and a daughter, Clara. John Poucher, from his photographs, was a short, stocky, sturdy-looking man with magnificent mutton chop whiskers and later a well-trimmed white beard, who worked as a Horncastle corn merchant.

We know very little about Poucher's ancestry, apart from a fascinating cutting which he kept in his scrapbook from the *Horncastle News* of 28 January 1933, which may refer to a distant relative. It refers back to a notorious burglary that took place at Horsted Hall, the home of Mr W. Elsey, near Woodhall Spa, in February 1829. At the time, it was described as 'one of the most daring burglaries ever committed in the county of Lincolnshire'.

Central to the plot was a character known as Richard Poucher, alias Slender Dick or Fiddler Sam, who was described as a 'banker and excavator' – presumably he was a canal navigator, or 'navvy', and excavated banks (of earth). Apparently, Poucher was the leader of a gang of six to eight men, disguised and armed with pistols, who burst into the hall that evening. After threatening to blow the servants' brains out, Poucher then held a pistol to Mr Elsey's head and demanded to know where he kept his plate. The gang carried away a variety of articles to the value of about £400.

After a reward had been offered, three members of the gang were swiftly apprehended, tried and executed in Lincoln Castle. But despite a nationwide search, Poucher and a couple of the others remained at large until the ringleader was arrested about six weeks later at a public house in Boston, Lincolnshire, where he was again working on a canal navigation, by two armed officers from Marlborough Street Police Station in London.

A violent struggle resembling a Wild West shoot-out then took place between the officers and the other navvies, estimated to number about a hundred men, in the pub, but the policemen managed to escape in a post chaise and took the prisoner with them back to Horncastle. He was instantly identified by Mr Elsey, as he had been his servant about twelve years before, and had threatened to get his revenge after he had been dismissed. Poucher was tried at the next Lincoln Assizes, and followed his compatriots to the gallows.

In later years, Walter Poucher attributed his good health and longevity to his upbringing in the 'wide open spaces of Lincolnshire'. Asked what was the secret of his fitness in a newspaper interview in his eighty-seventh year, he replied: 'Luck in having the right ancestors and fresh air.' But it was the contrasting drama of the mountains compared with the place where he was born and brought up which first fascinated Poucher. In the same interview, he said: 'Coming from the flatlands of England, it was a new world for me.'

He said in a profile published in *The Climber* in May 1965 that this instinctive love of mountains had also been sparked by his interest in photography. He had begged his father to take him for a holiday in the Lake District so that he could climb the fells, only to be told that he should first gain some experience on the slightly less than mountainous Lincolnshire Wolds. In those days, the family took their holidays at the seaside every year, in places like Scarborough on the Yorkshire coast. It was not until 1912 that he finally achieved that long-held ambition of visiting the Lake District.

Young William (he was also sometimes known in the family as Arthur, and wasn't known as Walter until he picked up the nickname during his Army service) attended the local primary and grammar schools in Horncastle. We have no record of his academic achievements at Queen Elizabeth's Grammar School, Horncastle, under the apparently formidable headmaster Dr Madge,

A young Poucher in sailor suit, aged about three.

'Granny Poucher,' Walter's mother, Rachel.

but as it was always in his nature to excel in whatever he did, there is no reason to doubt that he was anything but a model pupil.

Young Poucher attended piano lessons from the age of eight and became a very accomplished player, giving several public concerts from the age of twelve in Horncastle and Midlands. Like everything else he did, he wanted to be the best so he practised constantly. Before he left school he could play the majority of Chopin's works from memory. In an interview by Ivan Rowan in the *Sunday Telegraph* in 1983, he recalled how his marathon practice sessions of up to six hours every day had to be curtailed by his father: 'He had to turn the gaslight off at midnight to get me to go to bed,' explained Poucher.

Like many other pianists, he was particularly fond of the works of Chopin, Liszt and Rachmaninov. His favourite pianist was the Russian maestro Anton Rubinstein, and his favourite piece of music was Liszt's majestic *B Minor Sonata*. Rowan asked him in the same interview if he had ever played it and Poucher replied: 'Oh no, it was technically much too difficult,' and he went on to explain, in a rare burst of humility, why he had abandoned the role of a virtuoso: 'I have been a perfectionist all my life. I don't think I was good enough.'

Poucher later claimed he had been dissuaded from a career in music by his father, who shattered the small boy's musical ambitions in much the same way as he did his desire to climb mountains. He told him that there were so many pianists around he would most probably end up as a church organist giving lessons to children in some anonymous small country town. Poucher once described this possible scenario as 'a lifetime of piano lessons and village hall organs'. That would certainly not have been good enough for him.

His son John recalled him still constantly practising at home on his Steinway even in his later years. 'I remember lying in bed upstairs while father was practicing on the piano in the sitting room below and hearing him stop and use a mild invective when he made a mistake – this was sometimes repeated several times,' recalled John. 'Although he was an accomplished player, mistakes were still possible.' Poucher continued to enjoy playing the piano as a hobby, and didn't sell his prized Steinway until 1958 when he was sixty-seven.

After he left school, although he apparently initially harboured an idea that he wanted to be a carpenter, Poucher served a traditional four-year apprenticeship as a pharmacist with Messrs Carlton and Sons, the local Horncastle manufacturing chemists. Carlton's had been established in 1858 and their shop was at 8 Horncastle High Street. They had another shop at Woodhall Spa, where Poucher also served for a season. Carlton's also doubled as portrait and landscape photographers as many chemists did in those days, so the young apprentice may well have had an early introduction into the mysteries of glass plate photography and the darkroom with them. Later, Poucher converted a small cupboard at the head of the cellar steps of the family home in Queen Street into his own makeshift darkroom.

He described his first employer to Frank Haley in an interview in *The Chemist and Druggist* in 1961 as 'a fine example of the old-style apprentice master, very dignified, wearing top hat, white gloves and other impressive attire, and the conductor of the local orchestra'. He also praised the system

Signed portrait of Poucher as a young man-about-town, c.1914.

that had meant he had to pass a preliminary examination before being accepted as an apprentice. In a letter to *The Pharmaceutical Journal and Pharmacist* in 1916, he wrote: 'I have often admired the gentleman to whom I was apprenticed on that ground. He would never take an apprentice until he had passed his Prelim. How many pharmacists are there in Great Britain who take up that position today?'

The immaculate, sartorially elegant appearance of his first boss might also have had a lasting effect on the young Poucher, who in later life became well known for exactly the same kind of pride in his own spic and span appearance. We can also imagine that Mr Carlton's obvious love of music would have struck a sympathetic chord with the young Poucher.

It was Carltons who produced many of the earliest card-backed photographs in the Poucher family album, including a charming one of the young William, who then could have been no more than three years old, dressed in naval uniform complete with kilt, petticoat and sailor's hat bearing the name 'Sultan', and standing on a cushion so he could reach the arm of a chair. The chubby face and piercing blue eyes look quizzically at the cameraman as if he is taking it all in.

There are also several studio portraits of his mother Rachel, looking quite severe with brushed back hair and wearing the fashionable black dress of the time, complete with a prominent bustle. A splendid family group taken in September 1896, shows the blond four-year-old William in a velvet suit standing proudly between his maternal grandmother, Esther Dixon, and his father John, who rests a protective hand on his shoulder. Also in the stiffly posed photograph, apparently taken in the garden of the Dixon house, are Poucher's mother Rachel, looking regal in a puff-sleeved dress, maternal grandfather Charles Dixon, uncle Arthur Dixon, and younger sister Clara.

While he may have enjoyed the photographic side of the business, it is easy to imagine the frustration he might have felt listening to the symptoms and then doling out pills and other prescriptions to the worthy townsfolk of Horncastle. All the while he must have been harbouring deep inside the intense ambition to make a name for himself, which was to become so evident in his later years. He could very well have felt the same kind of irritation so vividly described by H.G. Wells in his 1910 humorous novel *The History of Mr Polly*, which was based on the life of a fictional Edwardian small town shopkeeper. And although he never fashioned such a dramatic denouement as did Alfred Polly, Poucher may well have sympathised with his feelings such as when he famously described 'Fishbourne' in the opening lines of the novel as a 'Beastly Silly Wheeze of a Hole!' We know that Poucher seems to have had no great love for the 'flatlands' of his early surroundings.

After his four-year apprenticeship with Carltons, Poucher spent six months with Mr W.E. Gould of Teddington, Middlesex. But he knew that if he were to pursue a career in pharmacy, he needed to qualify. So he attended the Bath and West of England College of the Pharmaceutical Society in Bath in 1912, to study for the qualifying examination, winning the bronze medal of the society for his aggregate marks in his PhC 'Minor' test in 1913, and gaining his 'Major' in July of the same year.

The elegant surroundings of the Georgian town on the banks of the Avon in Somerset were a far cry from sleepy Horncastle, and Poucher must have enjoyed the intellectual challenge of studying for his qualification in such surroundings. Poucher later became interested in medicine and, after attending King's College in London, where he read Medicine and Pharmacy, briefly toyed with the idea of becoming a doctor.

After qualification, he joined the staff of Allen and Hanburys Ltd, pharmaceutical chemists in London, and as the clouds of war gathered over Europe, Poucher joined the patriotic rush to serve his King and Country in December 1914. While still a civilian, he had taken charge of medical stores and dispensaries in the Eastern Command of the Army. His life-changing Army career is described in greater detail in the following chapter.

Romance had bloomed when Poucher met, courted and married Hilda Mary Coombes, who hailed from the former cloth manufacturing town of Gillingham, lying under the southern edge of Salisbury Plain on the northern borders of Dorset where it rises to meet Somerset and Wiltshire. The ancient bridge over the Shreen Water in the middle of Gillingham was the subject of a painting by John Constable which now hangs in London's Tate Britain, and the Coombes lived at the rather grand Newbury House in the village.

We don't know how or where the couple met – perhaps it was when Poucher was studying for his PhC in Bath. Poucher's son John recalled that his mother came from a big family. In fact, she had five sisters, Olivia, Jessica, Herminie, Rosemary and Doris, and a brother, William. Hilda's mother remarried into the Maloney family, who were well known as soap-makers in Gillingham, specialising in toilet and household products. Among their prize-winning soaps were 'Extermo', described as 'The People's Carbolic', and 'Dispello', famed for dispelling dirt. Two postcards in the Poucher family album show a stand of the Maloney Soap Co. Ltd. at a show, and a mobile horse-drawn wagon, perhaps prepared for a local carnival, advertising their wares.

Photographs of Hilda from the family album show her to be a lady with a mischievous glint in her eye and the ghost of a smile flickering across her lips. She looks as if she was someone with a sense of humour, perhaps inherited from her Irish ancestors, and maybe she needed it. Hilda obviously got on well with Poucher's siblings as there is a series of photographs

taken on a rocky, pebble-strewn beach –
perhaps on the coast of her native Dorset –
showing Hilda evidently having a happy
time with a group which includes Clara,
Poucher's young sister, and Poucher
himself.

The Christmas card – literally just
a postcard – she sent to her parents at
Newbury House, Gillingham, in 1910
is in the 'Kute Pets' series and shows a
cartoon of a slyly winking tomcat out
on the tiles, licking his lips and singing
to a silhouetted female on a neighbouring
rooftop: 'I hear you calling me.' Another
photograph, perhaps taken to mark the
couple's engagement, shows a Poucher family

ABOVE: Hilda Poucher
(née Maloney) as a
young woman.

LEFT: Hilda Poucher's
maternal step-parents
were soap-makers in
Gillingham, Dorset. This
was the Maloney's Soap
Co's carnival float.

Hilda and Walter
Pocher on the steps of
the Wesleyan
Methodist Central
Methodist Hall,
Westminster, London,
after their wedding on
18 February 1919.

group with both Poucher and his brother Charles in military uniform
flanked by their parents, John and Rachel, with sister Clara at one end and
Hilda, obviously showing off her engagement ring and seated at the left
(See page 32).

The couple were married at the Wesleyan Methodist Central Methodist Hall, Westminster, London, on 18 February 1919, when Poucher was still a captain in the Royal Army Medical Corps and recently returned from three years' service on the Western Front in France. The wedding certificate gives his address as the Hotel Rubens, Buckingham Palace Road and Hilda's as Newbury House, Gillingham. Their wedding photograph taken by a London photographic agency shows them standing arm in arm on the steps of the Central Hall, Hilda carrying a large bunch of flowers and wearing a broad-brimmed hat and long straight velvet-trimmed dress. Poucher is complete in puttees with a brightly-polished Sam Browne belt, marking his status as a commissioned officer.

The formal family wedding photograph (page 32) shows the couple seated and flanked by Hilda's rather stern looking parents, with Poucher's sister Clara in the back row with Hilda's sisters Olivia and Jessica. There is no sign of Poucher's parents or his brother Charles, but perhaps it was difficult to get from Horncastle to London so shortly after the end of the war.

A postcard from Colwyn Bay sent in August 1919 – perhaps while they were on their honeymoon – is cheekily addressed to 'The Squire of Gillingham' and is apparently in Poucher's handwriting but signed 'Arthur' (his middle name) and, rather intriguingly, by 'the pair that ran away'. A photographic postcard of Snowdon from across Llyn Llydau (*sic*) from the same holiday predates Poucher's classic view of the subject and the message written by Hilda on the back shows that the newlyweds had ascended the mountain by the railway (something Poucher would surely have scorned in later years) 'on a fairly clear day at last' and had lunch at the Summit Restaurant, from where the franking mark shows that they sent the card to her grandparents in Dorset.

The marriage seems to have been a happy one and the young couple were blessed with a son, whom they named John Bernard, in 1920. Photographs of John, a chubby baby with the same steely blue eyes of his father, with his mother show her obvious love and affection for the child. Another photograph sent from 'Hilda and Jack' to Poucher on his thirtieth birthday in

RIGHT: Poucher's paternal family, taken sometime during his war service. Left to right: Hilda Poucher (wife), John Poucher (father), Charles Poucher (brother), WAP, Rachel Poucher (mother) and Clara Poucher (sister).

BELOW: Walter and Hilda's wedding day, 18 February 1919. Left to right: unknown bridesmaid, Mr Coombes (Hilda's father), Clara Poucher (WAP's sister), Hilda Poucher, possibly Hilda's brother William, WAP, Olivia Coombes (Hilda's sister), Mrs Coombes (Hilda's mother) and another unknown bridesmaid.

Walter and Hilda with son John.

November 1921 shows Hilda standing rather primly in a conservatory, and the message in her handwriting on the back reads: 'You once asked for a photograph of me, this is one my sister took at Easter.'

John's relationship with his father from the beginning was a distant and quite a cold one. He showed little outward affection to his young son, unless it happened that their interests coincided. 'He was a hard man,' John confessed to me. 'If he had an ambition, he would go for it. Everything else, including his family, became incidental. He wanted to excel in everything that he did. And of course he mostly succeeded in those ambitions.' That view was echoed by John's son, Tony (Poucher's grandson), who said: 'Gramps could not be called a lovable man, in fact he could be quite ruthless and would stamp on anyone who stood in the way of his ambition.'

An example of that Edwardian coldness and inability to convey any sign of affection occurred when John was about ten years old and he accompanied his father on a trip to Snowdonia. They were ascending the serious knife-edge ridge of Crib Goch on the eastern flank of Snowdon when they came to a place where it was necessary to have a long reach to negotiate a bad step.

ABOVE: Hilda with John Poucher, their son.

ABOVE RIGHT: A studio portrait of a rather portly WAP with young son John.

'My arms were just not long enough to reach the hold,' recalled John. 'After trying for some time I gave up the attempt and burst into tears while my father just looked on. Shortly afterwards, two other climbers arrived and without more ado hoisted me up between them and placed me on the other side of the obstacle. My tears were soon forgotten and we went merrily on our way.'

On mountain walks, John was often asked to pose by his father to provide the foreground for a photograph. 'He used to complain about the time I had to stand or sit waiting until the light was just to his liking. I often used to slake my thirst from mountain streams on these trips, and he observed that while I took on liquid, he often needed to do the reverse.'

A Camera in the Hills

Poucher bought his son a camera when he was still quite young, and encouraged him to use it to the best of his ability. In later years, he passed on to John some of his old Leicas when he acquired newer models. 'When walking with him on the fells, I sometimes took pictures from the same viewpoints as father, and when they were developed and printed we compared them, mainly to see what difference was shown by the quality of the lenses in the two cameras.'

John recalled: 'If I had managed to get a decent shot he would say "You're learning, boy" – which was an encouragement and praise indeed!'

So highly did Leica think of Poucher's constant promotion in his books of their 'miniature' cameras, that when the new LeicaFlex model came out, they sent him one as a gift, with 28mm and 50mm lenses. 'Apparently the only other person who was sent one as a present was the Queen,' recalled grandson Tony Poucher. 'And then Gramps had the brass neck to ask them for another, 135mm telephoto lens, which they duly sent.'

But there was also a certain level of double standards at work within the Poucher psyche, recalled John. 'Although he often complained about people who discarded rubbish on the fells, he himself frequently threw away the cellophane wrappers which enclosed his Hamlet cigars. When I mentioned this he would say airily, "Don't worry, it will just blow away."' That self-centred nature of Poucher also made itself felt when John, then still a schoolboy at Seaford College, failed to remember his father's birthday one year. 'Believe it or not,' said John, 'I was made to write out lines stating that I would not commit this oversight again.'

John would eventually follow in his father's footsteps, entering the perfume business and becoming managing director and later chairman of the British distribution company of the French perfumers, Roure Bertrand Dupont, based at Harefield, Middlesex.

The young family had moved to Surrey in 1923 to be closer to Poucher's work in London, living first in a house on Epsom Downs and later to another in Ewell. But the happiness of the marriage with Hilda was to be short-lived and tragedy struck just five years later when she died at the young age of thirty-three on 7 August 1924, while giving birth to a still-born daughter. The funeral card described Hilda as the 'dearly beloved wife' of Poucher and carried the elegy:

> A memory that will not fade,
> A love that cannot die,
> Is with thee in thy rest
> In the home beyond the sky.

Hilda was interred in the churchyard of the fourteenth-century parish church of St Mary her family home of Gillingham in Dorset on 11 August 1924.

Poucher's second wife, Elsie Dorothy Wood – known in the family as 'Auntie Didi' – had been his housekeeper for many years, and was the daughter of engineer John Edward Wood. The couple moved into a splendid tile-fronted, steeply gabled house called Courtlands at Kingswood, in the heart of the lovely native woodland known as The Warren, in Surrey in

The memorial card for Hilda Poucher, who died in childbirth on 7 August 1924.

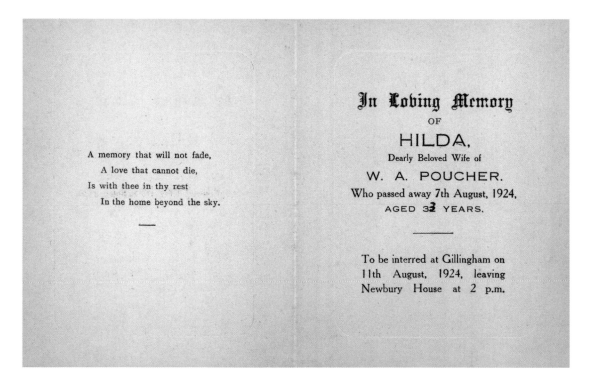

A memory that will not fade,
A love that cannot die,
Is with thee in thy rest
In the home beyond the sky.

In Loving Memory
OF
HILDA,
Dearly Beloved Wife of
W. A. POUCHER.
Who passed away 7th August, 1924,
AGED 33 YEARS.

To be interred at Gillingham on 11th August, 1924, leaving Newbury House at 2 p.m.

1929. They actually married eight years later at Kensington Register Office on 11 June 1937, when Poucher was forty-five and Dorothy thirty-nine. He gave his address as the Gardens Hotel, Palace Gate, London, and Dorothy gave hers as the Spencer House Hotel, Palace Gate.

Courtlands was close to the Surrey heathlands on which Dorothy loved to ride her horses, and to the prestigious Walton Heath Golf Club, where Poucher was an enthusiastic member. He liked to play at least nine holes every day when he was at home and, at the height of his golfing prowess, boasted a highly-respectable handicap of eleven. Poucher often lunched at the club restaurant, where he would occasionally entertain guests. He was particularly proud of two photographs which he had taken of the course which were hung on the clubroom wall.

Poucher explained his and Dorothy's love of the 'seclusion and sylvan charm' of Kingswood in *The Surrey Hills* (1949) – a book which was dedicated to the veteran professional and five times British Open winner James Braid and his fellow members of the Walton Heath Golf Club:

We soon grew to love its dainty silver birches, fine old Scots pines and the masses of rhododendrons that splash the whole neighbourhood with colour in the late spring. There was also another attraction in the proximity of Walton Heath where my wife could ride to her heart's content whilst I walked over the windswept, heathery downs. In addition excel-

A studio portrait of WAP's second wife, Dorothy (*née* Woods).

RIGHT: Courtlands, Kingswood, Surrey, shortlived home of Walter and Dorothy.

ABOVE: Parkside Lodge, Reigate, WAP's home after the move from Courtlands.

lent golf was to be had on its two first class courses where healthy exercise and good companionship add spice to the playtime of life.

John Poucher recalled that his father was highly accomplished as a golfer, as he was in most things he did, and arranged for him to have lessons when he was quite young. 'But I was never up to his standard,' he confessed to me. In later years, John sometimes had a game with his father at Walton Heath, and he recalled one incident at the eighteenth hole. 'On this occasion my ball landed in a very deep bunker. Such was my ineptitude that I thrashed away for some time without managing to hit the ball out, while my

A Camera in the Hills

LEFT: Dorothy with two of her beloved pets, the Pekinese dog known as Kiki, and a budgerigar.

BELOW LEFT: Dorothy and pet dog on the lawn of Courtlands.

BELOW: Spring time at Courtlands.

The extended Poucher family, showing (standing left to right): WAP, Hilda Poucher (sister-in-law), John Poucher (son), Clara Poucher (sister), Hannah Brison (Hilda's mother), Charles Poucher (brother); (seated left to right): Dorothy Poucher (second wife), Anthony Poucher (grandson) and Olivia Coombes (sister-in-law from his first marriage).

father waited patiently on the green, with a rather bored expression on his face. My son Tony, who was with us, nearly had hysterics!'

The couple later moved to the equally-baronial Parkside Lodge, in Crescent Road, Reigate, another tile-fronted mock-Tudor manor house in the heart of Surrey. Although he loved to be in the mountains, Poucher also obviously loved his creature comforts at home, and the couple lived in relative luxury in one of the most expensive and exclusive parts of London's Green Belt. Dorothy kept a pampered Pekinese dog known as Kiki, and a budgerigar. In later years, they moved into a first-floor apartment at 'Heathfield', the palatial former home of film mogul J. Arthur Rank, in Reigate Heath, Surrey, which had been converted into several luxurious apartments.

Poucher rarely smiled in photographs, but here he is seen enjoying a joke with his young son, John.

The summer of 1930 was marred by a tragic accident while Poucher was travelling through Weston near Honiton in Devon towards Exeter on a hot summer Saturday in June, when the car he was driving skidded on the hot tarmac and knocked down and killed a six-year-old boy. The boy, Stanley George Mullins of Hamlet Cottages, Weston, received a fractured skull and brain injuries and died later that day at home after suffering convulsions.

At the inquest held in Exeter four days later, Poucher volunteered to give evidence and explained to the jury that the lad had suddenly, without looking, run across the road, hesitated, and had then run on. The car was travelling at no more than 35 miles per hour when he saw the boy, about 20 or 30 feet away. He immediately braked and swerved to avoid him, but the car skidded on the semi-liquid road surface, and the boy disappeared under

the bonnet of the car, which ended up in the hedge. Poucher explained that he had been driving for five or six years, and had covered 50,000 miles mainly in the suburbs of London and had never had an accident before. After what the Exeter *Express and Echo* described as a lengthy deliberation, the jury returned a verdict of accidental death, and exonerated the driver from all blame.

Poucher never lost his love of fast, expensive cars, particularly favouring Jaguar and Alvis models, which often later appeared in the foreground of the few roadside photographs he took in the hills. He later moved on to a Triumph Dolomite Sprint and a BMW, which he continued to drive at high speeds, despite the loss of the sight in his right eye.

But we have jumped ahead in the Poucher story and we must now return to the dark days of the First World War, to trace Poucher's four-year career in the Royal Army Medical Corps, and discover how it was to change his life forever, and turn him against a career in medicine.

WAP perfects his golf swing at Walton Heath.

A Camera in the Hills

Surrey Hills: Birches at
Walton Heath.

3. PHOTOGRAPHER AT WAR

The Somme is a name that stands as the epitome of senseless slaughter and the embodiment of the futility of trench warfare. The battle lasted five months between July and November 1916 and was fought by around two million men on a thirty-mile front between Amiens and Peronne in north-western France. The much-vaunted 'Big Push' masterminded by the British commander Sir Douglas Haig, which aimed to break through the obdurate German lines, ground to a sickening halt in the choking, cloying Flanders mud. While it produced no strategic gain, it did produce over one million casualties of whom the Allied total was 600,000, two-thirds of them British. On the first day alone (1 July 1916) the British Army lost 57,470 men, 19,240 of them killed and 2,152 missing – making it easily the bloodiest day in its long history.

It seems it was his service as a field pharmacist in the 41st Casualty Clearing Station on the Western Front which finally turned Poucher against a career in medicine. In an interview with Jim Crumley in *The Great Outdoors* in April 1981, Poucher admitted in a rare cathartic moment that it was the first-hand horrors he witnessed of the results of trench warfare at Ypres and on the Somme that had made up his mind. Crumley noted that even sixty years after the event and then in his ninetieth year, his face screwed up tight at the still-vivid memory as he briefly recalled: 'Piles of arms and legs, people suffering agonies . . . ' He told Crumley that it was enough for him to decide against medicine for ever.

It was while Poucher was attending a lecture at St Bartholomew's Hospital in 1914 in the first year of the Great War that a colonel from the War Office made an appeal for chemists, who were urgently needed at the Front. Poucher was in his early twenties at this time, and the appeal must have hit home with him as it did with thousands of other patriotic young men, because he offered himself immediately at Chelsea Barracks as a

OPPOSITE: WAP in Army greatcoat, ready for war.

A Camera in the Hills

dispenser with the Royal Army Medical Corps, only to be told that all vacant positions were filled and that he would be doing more useful work staying where he was.

Undaunted, he sent his name in to the War Office and two months later was employed, for 6s (30p) a day plus rations and quarters, as a civilian dispenser in a military hospital just outside London. He recalled in an address on his Army service to the British Pharmaceutical Conference in 1919: 'Like a good many more enthusiasts, the question of rank and pay was not even considered so long as I had the opportunity of doing something useful towards beating the Germans in the conjectured six months. In the event, he was to serve for three long years in France.

In December, 1914, Poucher was sent to the RAMC training hospital at Purfleet in Surrey, which was a converted school where the cloakroom served as a dispensary. It was here that Poucher first met the situation as he would later in France, where completely unqualified personnel were being employed as dispensers by the Army. In the same conference address, Poucher recalled meeting an old Army colour sergeant who previous to the War had been 'engaged in work anything but pharmaceutical', but who was now serving as a dispenser and preparing and handing out two or three bottles of medicine a day, and occasionally dressing a cut finger.

'I found this gentleman most entertaining,' said Poucher, 'and what he did not know about "jerking the column" or "swinging the lead", as Army phraseology has it, was not worth knowing. But, on his own admission, he knew little, if anything, of pharmacy.'

Poucher was eventually commissioned as a Lieutenant Quartermaster with the RAMC in November 1915, but only after he had made another personal approach to the War Office. Within ten days he found himself on the Western Front in France attached to the 41st Casualty Clearing Station.

We have a first-hand account of Poucher's journey to France. Before he was commissioned, he had started writing regularly in the *The Pharmaceutical Journal and Pharmacist* on subjects like 'The Modern

Military Hospital' and signing himself 'Civilian Dispenser'. Busy as ever, he continued with his contributions from the thick of the action in France, under the anonymous byline 'Lieutenant RAMC'.

In the first of these contributions, dated 15 January 1916, he describes his discovery that he was the only qualified dispenser in the unit and his journey across the English Channel to France to spend his first Christmas of the war there.

> We embarked early and, being the first unit on board our transport, I had the novel experience of being made QM of the ship during the voyage, which, fortunately, proved to be a short one. After the numerous odd units had made themselves as comfortable as possible down below, we sailed; and what a voyage too, in a rough sea, with twenty-eight officers to occupy four bunks!
>
> Of course, seniority had priority, and some of us juniors had to make ourselves comfortable on the mess room floor. One would suddenly wake with a man treading on one's legs in his hasty endeavours to reach the ship's side to get rid of some uncomfortable interior 'packing'.

The company disembarked at seven o'clock the next morning in France, and marched five miles into the countryside to what was laughingly called 'a rest camp' at Le Havre. As Poucher remarked, the term 'rest camp' sounded attractive, but it was far from that, as they were soon to learn.

> On arrival we found it was a field set apart entirely for the encampment of casualty clearing stations, three of which had been there for some weeks. We made ourselves fairly 'comfy' in tents, with the rain coming down in sheets and about six inches of mud on the ground. However, it is surprising how one accommodates oneself to one's surroundings, and in a few days we began to feel quite at home.

Poucher as the young RAMC officer, at about the time of his wedding in 1919.

Poucher found that the duties of a QM at a rest camp were anything but demanding, and included such mundane events as the signing of the ration book first thing every morning, and regular kit inspections. But he soon discovered he had a couple of other quite unexpected responsibilities. 'Of our cooks, two were entitled to 2d (about 1p) a day extra pay, and as there were four aspirants, the colonel appointed me as examiner,' he wrote in his column in *The Pharmaceutical Journal and Pharmacist*. 'For half a day I had to swat hard at the composition of such things as rice puddings, beef tea, and scrambled eggs, and then the four men were paraded for examination. With some little difficulty I managed to find the two best men, and they consequently got their 2d a day advance.'

The task he was given a few days later was a bit more to his liking. He was charged with examining the three dispensers who were serving in the unit, as the Commanding Officer had evidently begun to doubt their abilities. The tests started with an oral examination in prescription reading. Poucher was mortified at the results. Not only were the men untrained – one had been a clerk with a firm of wholesale chemists and the other two were porters – they were also potential killers. 'Within five minutes I proved the ignorance of these gentry to be appalling, for they failed to note such overdoses as one drachm of Liq. Strychnin.'

His resultant report to his CO was apparently 'very terse'. 'As far as I could judge,' he was to write later, '[they were] totally incompetent to take charge of our pharmaceutical branch.' Within a fortnight, a staff sergeant compounder arrived much to Poucher's, and presumably the CO's, relief.

He never forgot this experience or the previous one he had at the Purfleet training hospital, and resolved to strive his hardest to do something to rectify the situation. After his demobilisation in 1918, Poucher began a vigorous campaign to get all RAMC dispensers properly trained and commissioned, and to introduce a full-blown Pharmaceutical Service within the RAMC. He started on a nationwide lecture tour of local branches of the Pharmaceutical Society based on the address he had given to the British Pharmaceutical Conference in 1919. And judging from the cuttings he kept in his scrapbook, he was successful in grabbing the headlines in the regional press. Stories about Tommies being dosed with poisons by unqualified blacksmiths, porters and railwaymen while other trained pharmacists were used as orderlies, and about the system being in a 'hopeless mess', filled many column inches in local newspapers as far apart as Cambridge, Nottingham, Croydon, Swansea and Blackburn.

In a leader following the report headed 'Queer Tales of How Our

Tommies Were Dosed', on Poucher's address to the Nottingham Pharmaceutical Society on 11 February 1925, the *Nottingham Journal* commented: 'The report of last night's meeting reads like a chapter from the history of the Crimean War.'

Christmas 1915 approached while Poucher was still at the rest camp at Le Havre with no sign of a move to the Front Line, so the company (presumably Poucher himself, who as we know was an accomplished pianist) hired a piano in preparation for the festivities. Poucher described the celebrations in an article: 'We gave the men a concert on Christmas Eve, which they enjoyed, and we continued our merrymaking until past midnight. Christmas Day was quiet, as was the ensuing week, but the men had another concert on New Year's Eve, which was rather more exciting than the previous one. We saw the arrival of the New Year, joining hands over *Auld Lang Syne*.'

Things were apparently not quite so jolly for one company, who had the misfortune to receive their marching orders on 31 December and found themselves in cattle trucks for the dawning of the New Year. Otherwise, Poucher said the only bright spot in their lives was the arrival of the post from home, which included the weekly *Pharmaceutical Journal*. He added: 'We are all eagerly awaiting for our orders to move up the line.' That order did not come until early in 1916, as preparations were proceeding for the start of the fateful Battle of the Somme.

Immediately, Poucher applied for a qualified man to relieve the untrained sergeant compounder in the dispensary, and after a few days a private from his home county of Lincolnshire arrived who was a chemist and druggist. Poucher tried valiantly to have this man promoted, but could only get him raised to lance-corporal (unpaid). We don't know the name of this man, but Poucher obviously had a high regard for him and was deeply saddened when he was killed one night during the Battle of Arras in April 1917 – within half an hour of his returning to the front from a period of leave.

Poucher described the preparations for setting up of the 41st Casualty Clearing Station before this battle, which started on Easter Monday 1917 with a seven-hour bombardment of the German front. Because of the necessity of keeping troop movements secret, orders were given that tents were not be be pitched until a few days before zero hour. At the time, the 41st were stationed at Wanquetin, but the first intimation of the attack came in January 1917. They were given the map location of their new site just behind the town of Arras and, on a freezing winter's day, Poucher set out with his colonel to view their new home. 'We found a ploughed field, with a stream at the back and odd ammunition dumps near by, with the whole area about four inches deep in snow. This was (not) what one might call a cheerful outlook, and we proceeded to map out the area and search for a water supply.'

They had permission to erect huts which, they were told, would not attract the attention of the German Air Force because they would appear like permanent structures. But the unit was told that they would have to obtain the huts themselves from an area further back, pull them down, transport and then re-erect them on the new site. Poucher recounts how after a long search, he discovered a dilapidated former cowshed and how, under cover of darkness, they dismantled it and transported it in lorries for re-erection on the new site to serve as the new dispensary. It was painted with a whitewash they made up from the local chalk.

During the final German push of 1918, Poucher admitted: 'Pharmacy in the early years of the retreat was almost a negligible factor owing to the rapid advance of the Germans.'

> We retired at the rate of fifteen to twenty miles a day, with practically no equipment, as we had left almost everything behind. We rendered as much assistance as we could to other medical units in our rear, and at the end of a week found ourselves in an orchard south of Amiens, with a lull in the fighting. . . . We settled down in our orchard, found some marquees, and proceeded to do our best for the wounded, who were coming down in hundreds. We gave the dispenser a small marquee and by nightfall, he had obtained some dressings and we were carrying on to the best of our ability.

I shall never forget the horrors of the next seven days, because with only about forty marquees we treated no less than 21,000 odd cases. We worked day and night and it rained incessantly the whole time.

The Allied advance which followed was more orderly, and the pharmaceutical service 'rendered yeoman service', according to Poucher. It was usual to move up one day and open the next when the dispensary, along with the whole unit, had to be ready.

Poucher mentions the peripatetic nature of the Casualty Clearing Stations in his July 1919 article in *The Pharmaceutical Journal*:

> The position of the CCS varied in distance from the front line from four to twenty miles, and was able to offer more thorough and prolonged treatment to the wounded, with the consequence that pharmaceutical work became a little more elaborate. The dispensary sometimes crystallised into a tent or a hut, while I have occasionally seen them in the classroom of a school – the latter of course being a luxury. . . . You will perhaps realise the difficulty in keeping a really smart dispensary when you are reminded that this unit was classified as a mobile one, and in the last year of the war moved as much as once every four to six weeks.

At this point, it may be worth describing the rather complex chain of medical establishments which processed the casualties from the Front Line, eventually to reach hospitals back home. We can follow the actual experiences of one of Poucher's fellow Lincolnshire soldiers, Private Tom Bluette, a former journalist for the *Grimsby Daily Telegraph* and a member of A Company, 1/5th Lincolns in the 138th Brigade, 46th (North Midland) Division.

On the last day of his trench tour, 14 May 1915, Bluette became the twenty-first member of his battalion to be wounded since the beginning of the month, two of whom lost their lives. His injury was unfortunate and followed an incident which today would be described as 'friendly fire'. A comrade in Bluette's platoon had been taking pot shots over the parapet and his rifle had a round still in the breach. Somehow it managed to fire as he was lifting it, and the bullet passed through Bluette's hand and thigh.

Bluette described in a letter the evacuation process that would become familiar to so many of Poucher's patients in the months ahead:

> I realised I had been accidentally shot. Aid was soon forthcoming. My clothes were cut away and bandages applied, while later my comrade, who was quite upset, offered his explanation and apologies. I was obliged to remain in the trench from 9 am until nightfall before I could be removed to the dressing station at the end of the communication trenches. Just before tea the Germans sent over a few shells that knocked over our parapet. This was, I must confess a very very trying time for me, as I felt the position very keenly.

Just as it became dark Bluette was carried away by two stretcher bearers. It was still a difficult journey and took three hours to complete, but Bluette eventually reached the Advanced Dressing Station (ADS) after several stops:

> Here I was tallied with a label stating name, regiment, particulars of wounds, and as my wounds had already been dressed, they despatched me to a field hospital near to our billets. I was detained here for one night and my wounds were again dressed and an injection against septic poisoning given. [The next morning] I was moved once more to a hospital about five miles further back, the chaplain visited each patient and offered assistance in informing relatives of their injuries. The next hospital was an extensive building where men were deposited from miles around. I was only kept here for the evening as only the serious cases are detained.

The 'dressing station' to which Bluette referred was a Regimental Aid Post (RAP). Front line units such as infantry battalions were only able to provide the most superficial medical care. Located near the front line, often in a support or reserve trench, they were attended by the Battalion Medical Officer and his orderlies and stretcher bearers. A wounded man would either make his own way if possible, or be carried there. The facilities were crude and often just sufficed to carry out light first aid, give the casualty a drink, or just pass him down the chain to the ADS.

Although the ADS was slightly better equipped than the RAP, it could still only provide very limited medical treatment. Wounds could be dressed and some emergency operations were carried out. In times of heavy fighting, the ADS would often be overwhelmed by the volume of casualties arriving. Often, badly wounded men had to lie in the open on stretchers for a considerable time.

The wounded man would eventually be passed on down the line to a Casualty Clearing Station (CCS), such as Poucher's 41st, often by the wagon transport of the Divisional Supply Column. Former London Transport open-topped buses, charabancs, and light and broad gauge railways were used to transport casualties. The CCS was the first large, relatively well-equipped, medical facility that a wounded man like Tom Bluette would have seen. Its role was to retain all serious cases that were unfit for further travel, treat and return slight cases, and evacuate all others. It was usually a tented camp, although in the static trench areas the accommodation would sometimes be in huts.

The stations were often grouped into clusters of two or three in a small area, usually a few miles behind the lines. A typical station could hold 1,000 casualties at any time, and each would admit between 15 and 300 cases, in rotation. At peak times of battle, as Poucher found, the CCSs were overflowing. Many serious operations, such as limb amputations, were carried out here. If the man had been lucky enough to be identified as being a 'Blighty case' (i.e. he could be sent home) he was sent directly to a port of embarkation.

The serious nature of many wounds was often beyond the medical facilities and skills of a CCS, and many of their positions are today marked by the acres of white crosses of the large military cemeteries that are such an abiding and moving feature of the modern landscape of northern France.

From the CCS, the casualty would be evacuated to a hospital. Once admitted, wounded Tommies like Tom Bluette stood a reasonable chance of survival. More than half were evacuated to the UK from a General or Stationary Hospital for further treatment or convalescence.

We are lucky to be able to witness some of the actual scenes which Poucher must have known from his service with the 41st CCS in France because it was vividly portrayed by a distinguished patient who ended up there. He was the famous American portrait painter John Singer Sargent, whose watercolour *The Interior of a Hospital Tent, 1918*, is now kept in the Imperial War Museum in London. By coincidence, another war artist, J. Hodgson Lobley (1878–1954), specially employed by the RAMC in the rank of sergeant to record their work, also portrayed the 41st Casualty Clearing Station in 1918. It is among the thirty-three of his paintings that are also kept in the Imperial War Museum.

On 24 September 1918, Sargent was near Peronne with the 4th Army Prisoners of War Transit Cage, which was where prisoners taken from the Front were held before sending them further back. Sargent made some sketches here, gathering material for perhaps his most famous painting *Gassed*, but while doing so caught a bad case of influenza, and was taken to the 41st Casualty Clearing Station near Roisel, where he stayed a week in a camp bed in the hospital tent.

His painting of that tent captures the haunting calmness of the first light of morning, with the wounded men with whom he shared his tent lined up in their rickety camp beds, which are lit by shafts of sunlight. In a letter to Mrs Isabella Stewart Gardner, Sargent described the horrors of the fitful nights he spent in that hospital tent, when sleep was either impossible or only gained in brief moments.

The Interior of a Hospital Tent (1918) by John Singer Sargent, painted when Sargent was a patient in Poucher's own unit.

. . . the accompaniment of groans of wounded, and the choking and coughing of gassed men . . . was a nightmare – it always seemed strange on opening one's eyes [the next morning] to see the level cots and the dimly-lit, long tent looking so calm, when one (had been) dozing in pandemonium.

In another of his contributions to *The Pharmaceutical Journal and Pharmacist* published in June 1916, Poucher describes the evacuation of the wounded from the trenches to the base hospital as 'one of the marvels of this war'. With typical military understatement, he describes the case of a man who had 'received a dose of shrapnel' which had broken his leg,

Hospital Tent, by J. Hodgson Lobley, showing the 41st Casualty Clearing Station.

but also hints at the chaotic situation caused by the incessant artillery bombardment.

The writer knows a dressing station which is at present situated in the underground laboratories of what was once a technical school. The town has suffered many severe bombardments, and the upper part of the school is now in ruins. In this case the evacuation to the field ambulance usually takes place under cover of darkness, as all the roads leading to the town are under fire during daylight. If a big action is in progress, divisional collecting stations are established between the advanced dressing stations and the field ambulance in

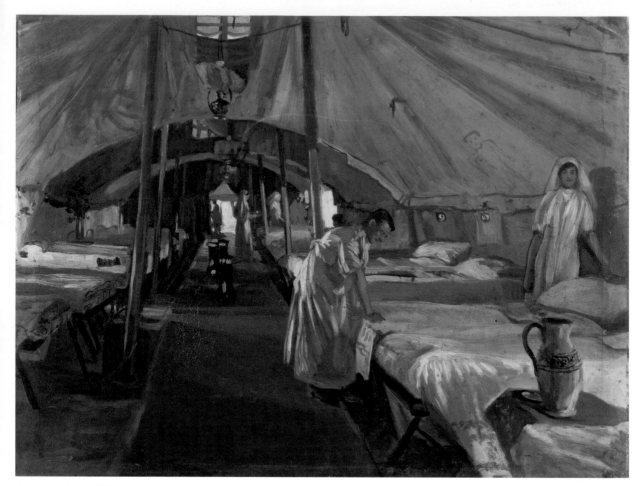

Another view of the 41st Casualty Clearing Station by John Singer Sergent.

order to equalise the number of cases sent to each ambulance and so avoid the possible 'choking up' of any particular line of evacuation.

In the same article Poucher says that 'very bad abdominal wounds' were despatched direct to the Casualty Clearing Station for immediate operation where two operating tables, plus a third improvised during a major action, were in use 'all working day and night'. One can only imagine the appalling conditions under which the doctors and surgeons had to work. In some cases they were so busy that lightly wounded men were given simple medical tasks to perform to relieve the pressure on the doctors.

An idea of the basic dignity and decency of the wounded is given in a story related in John Laffin's *On the Western Front* by a surgeon from Guy's

Hospital, London, who was serving with a CCS in a farm shed behind the Arras front line. There were no beds and the wounded men all lay close together on the floor. After kneeling for some time in an uncomfortable position while working on a dressing, the surgeon stood up and stepped back to stretch his back, and his foot touched another foot. There was a scream of agony but almost at once came a chorus from the other men lying on the floor. 'You didn't hurt him, sir. He often makes noises like that.' Another haggard soldier with three gaping wounds gripped his hand and whispered hoarsely: 'It *wasn't* your fault, sir.'

The surgeon reflected: 'Every man in the room took it for granted that my mental anguish for my stupidity was greater than his own physical pain, and was doing his best to deaden it for me.' And he posed the patriotically rhetorical question: 'In whose ranks are the world's greatest gentlemen?'

In another article in *The Pharmaceutical Journal* dated August 1916, Poucher, this time under the significantly anonymous byline 'Armiger', and perhaps in the light of his experience at the training and rest camps, wrote about the advisability of giving commissions to all qualified pharmacists serving in the RAMC. He asked:

> Would it be too much to expect the War Office to give commission rank to *all* qualified chemists acting as dispensers in the British Army, because, for field ambulances and casualty clearing stations, there are only two or three dispensers, and in the former almost all the drugs are in tablet form. . . . Why should not a British soldier who has risked his life for his country have his medicines dispensed by a trained man, the same as if he were in a civil hospital?

He concluded the hard-hitting article with a direct appeal to the later-to-be war coalition Prime Minister, David Lloyd George: 'Let us hope, with the advent of Mr Lloyd George at the War Office, we shall have our grievances rectified – much to the betterment of the medical service.'

In the next issue of the *Journal,* he backed his appeal with an outline of the situation as it applied in the French Army, where apparently all qualified pharmacists were commissioned officers. However, it appears that Poucher's campaign to commission chemists fell on stony ground because, although it was considered by the Progressive Pharmacy Club and a Special Committee, an Army Council Instruction issued early in 1919 came to the conclusion that while only trained pharmacists would be used by the RAMC on pharmaceutical work, they would nonetheless be precluded from receiving commissioned rank.

Poucher wrote a letter to the *Pharmaceutical Journal* on his demobilisation from the Army in April 1919:

> It is indeed unfortunate and regrettable, but I would remind those pharmacists still serving in the RAMC that although [this order] was published in wartime, it is an order which will apply to a peace time army, and as such the authorities are counting on your continued voluntary service. If their offer of NCOs rank, with its attractive [?] pay etc., is not sufficient to induce you to sign on as they anticipate, and there are in consequence no pharmacists to staff the hospitals in accordance with this order, what will they do?

In other wartime contributions to the *Journal*, Poucher also covered subjects as diverse as 'The Beet Sugar Industry of Northern France', 'The Industrial Value of the Potato' and the role and duties of the Quartermaster. By 1918, Poucher had been promoted to captain, and ever active, had submitted a scheme to the authorities for the reduction of transport on medical stores, and the establishment of pharmaceutical laboratories in the charge of properly trained officers.

Poucher finally left his unit in France in January 1919, and on his demobilsation, returned to England and to Lloyd George's 'land fit for heroes' with two new ambitions – to marry his sweetheart and to make his name in the world of cosmetic chemistry.

Like father, like son. WAP congratulates
John on his commission as 2nd
Lieutenant in the Royal Signals in 1941.

4. COSMETIC CHANGES:
THE SWEET SMELL OF SUCCESS

At the height of his powers as Britain's leading cosmetic chemist, Poucher was said to be able to carry the memory of 1,000 scents in his not inconsiderable nose. At this time he had been described as one of Britain's 'six secret tsars of beauty' and as one of the greatest living world authorities on cosmetics.

Andy MacFarlane, in his 'Man Talk' column in the *Toronto Sunday Telegraph* went even further with the nasal compliments when he interviewed Poucher, who was on a world tour for Yardley, on 7 April 1957. The owner himself of what he proudly described as a nose of 'heroic' proportions, he had been told that Poucher's was 'the greatest in the English speaking world'.

So he said he had mixed feelings when he learned that one of the world's great noses was coming to town, but soon discovered that Poucher's 'conk' had gained the unusual epithet not by virtue of its size, but its 'exquisite sensitivity and rigorous training'. When MacFarlane asked if he thought he could also follow his nose to fortune, Poucher replied: 'My dear sir, it isn't that one has a marvellous nose. One remembers odours. First, one recognises the characteristic odour of every single thing in the gamut of beautiful smells. Not only blossoms, but roots, stems, leaves and seeds. There are about 1,000 of them. And then there are all the synthetic aromatic chemicals.'

In a feature written by Hugh Cleland in the *London Evening Standard* on 4 January 1954, Poucher's nose was described as being 'as sensitive as a fine wine connoisseurs's palate'. Did drinking harm those amazing olfactory senses, Cleland wondered? Actually, the question did not arise; Poucher was a confirmed teetotaller. But he always enjoyed a fine cigar, and one wonders how that might have affected his nasal palate.

A studio shot of
Poucher the perfumer.

When MacFarlane had asked him how he had broken into the 'dollars-and-scents' business, Poucher gave him a potted history of how he entered the world of perfumery. With typical bonhomie, he boomed:

> My dear fellow, it's rather amusing really. I'd served in the First War with the Royal Army Medical Corps and afterwards, I didn't want to follow the usual routine work of science, for which I'd been trained. . . . So I spent years studying the chemistry of flower odours . . . all the beautiful smelling flowers . . . jasmine, lily of the valley, roses, and all the rest. Just when I was becoming expert, there was a greater demand for cosmetics. So I found myself in this extremely limited profession – there are only about half a dozen of us who actually create new odours from natural ingredients. And naturally, there are enormous rewards for those who have the perseverance to develop the interesting blend of science and art that is required.

Poucher had also told an interviewer for the *London Evening News* in 1938 that after the war, he'd looked around for a profession not already overcrowded, and saw that nobody in England had done much research in perfumery. Actually, Poucher had applied for the position of works manager with the United Chemists' Association Ltd (UCAL), a rapidly growing pharmaceutical manufacturing company with offices in Cheltenham, London and Liverpool, while still on active service in France.

When he arrived in his new post in at the firm's head office in Cheltenham early in 1919, he was given a free hand to organise and equip its plant for greatly increased production, especially of perfume and toilet preparations.

In his first editorial in the company magazine, *The Ucalite*, dated May 1919, the new works manager confessed he had been a 'Ucalite' since January 1917. 'At that time a good deal of experimental offensive gas warfare was being conducted by us south of Arras, and although it brought its casualties they were few and the days were long. Under these circumstances I looked forward to the arrival of my journal with perhaps more enthusiasm than I had done during my pre-war days.'

As for his own aspirations, and those of his new employers, he summarised them as follows: 'We desire to supply you with everything you require in your pharmacy – be it the elegant one of the residential quarter of a city or the unpretentious one of the working-class neighbourhood.' And with entirely typical bravado, he added: 'Some may think this ambitious – well – it is, but then what good do men do unless they are ambitious, and all Ucalites are ambitious and ought to be progressive.'

On a lighter note, Poucher seems to have enjoyed the social life associated with working within a large company. He penned and delivered a song entitled 'The UCAL Budget' at a dinner given by heads of departments in Cheltenham on St George's Day 1920, in honour of Harold Miller, who had recently returned from convalescent trip to Jamaica and the West Indies, and Miss E.S. Hooper, head of analytical control, who was retiring. Poucher presided over the dinner and entertainment, and also contributed two piano solos, playing Smetana's *Bohemian Dance* and the *Etude in C Major* by Chopin.

He brought in most leading members of staff into the sixteen verses of his satirical budget song, making fun of their individual idiosyncrasies. It included a verse about a long-serving pharmacist which seemed to echo Poucher's experiences in the RAMC:

> Wolstenholme of this Firm has seen many years,
> And the accuracy of his poisons he seldom has fears
> Into Gargle you ask him to put Strychnin for fun,
> When to Hades he'll consign you, at a very quick run.

And he concluded the song with a verse about himself:

> Now I am the last man who you'll criticise,
> For singing this song which tells so many lies,

But why worry about it and leave me in the lurch,
Just because I composed it last evening in church.

Poucher had become a prolific contributor of articles in the trade press both in this country, Europe and in the USA, covering subjects like 'Ancient and Modern Cosmetics and their Uses', 'New Perfumery Raw Materials', 'Floral Cachous' and 'Pearly Vanishing Creams'. It was while he was still working for UCAL that he realised there was a dearth of literature on the practical application of synthetics in perfumery. The last book on the subject had been written fifty years ago, and was now sadly out-of-date.

It was a gap he resolved to fill and the result was what is still regarded some eighty-five years later as the standard work on the subject. The first edition of *Perfumes and Cosmetics: with especial reference to synthetics*, was published by Chapman & Hall from its offices in Henrietta Street, London, in March 1923, with an initial print run of 2,000 copies. Chapman & Hall were the original publishers of the works of Charles Dickens and were also later to produce the first of Poucher's mountain photography books. The 474-page book, priced at 21s (£1.05), covered the production of natural perfumes, fixation, the manufacture of flower and fancy perfumes, toilet waters, bath, hair and dental preparations, lip slaves and rogue sticks, manicure preparations, skin creams and lotions, smelling salts, theatrical requisites and toilet powders.

The elegant dust jacket and cover design, with the title carefully scripted in calligraphy and with an illustration by Olive Shaw showing floral essences issuing from a heated, single-necked Woulfe bottle, is very much of its time, showing influences of the burgeoning Arts and Crafts movement.

The comprehensive reference work was written, according to the publicity, by 'a scientific perfumer . . . from a background of practical experience, much research, and the collaboration of men engaged in the industry.' In his preface, Poucher wrote:

The study of perfumes has a fascination unsurpassed by any other branch of chemistry. The researches of many distinguished scientists have gradually raised it from one of the minor arts almost to the level of a science.

Synthesis as a natural sequence follows analysis, and, whilst the synthetic perfumes at present evolved do not exactly reproduce the fragrance of the natural flower, they certainly attain a very close approximation, especially when blended artistically from flower absolutes.

And obviously with an eye to prospective sales, he added: 'There is also a pecuniary advantage to be gained by their employment, since they can also used successfully for perfuming cosmetics, soaps, etc., where price is often a very material consideration.'

Reviewers were unanimous in their praise for the comprehensive and long-awaited new reference book. The *Pharmaceutical Journal* wrote: 'Mr Poucher is to be congratulated on the production of undoubtedly one of the most useful books in the English language on the subject,' while the *Irish Chemist and Druggist* said: 'The author is to be congratulated on issuing so comprehensive a work, which will fill a long-felt want. . . . It is difficult to believe that anything of importance has been omitted, and the work should find a place on the bookself of every manufacturing chemist and retail pharmacist.'

The British *Chemist and Druggist* said: 'The book will appeal to the practical perfumer who really wants to know something about his work and the substances he uses in it . . . the book is distinctly good and contains a great deal of up-to-date, accurate matter within a reasonable compass. . . . We cordially recommend it to all interested in practical perfumery.' Professor Curt P. Wimmer in the *American Perfumer* said that they had recently called for a good book covering perfumes and cosmetics, and now their wish had been fulfilled. 'Poucher's book is a real good one. It is up-to-date, written in good style, and contains a great deal of valuable information. . . . Our opinion is that Poucher's *Perfumes and Cosmetics* is the best book on the subject published in the English language to date.'

After five seemingly happy years with UCAL in Cheltenham, Poucher resigned in 1924 to take up a new post as managing director of R.F. White Ltd, producers of toilet soaps and perfumery, in London. He subsequently acquired a controlling interest in the company but later disposed of it and opened his own consulting practice in Victoria Street, Westminster. Significantly among his earliest clients was Yardley of London.

A second edition of his master work, revised and enlarged into two volumes but with the same title appeared in 1925. The first volume, which ran to 314 pages and was priced at 16s (80p), contained a dictionary of raw materials; the second volume cost 21s (£1.05) for its 422 pages, and was subtitled *A Treatise on Practical Perfumery*. Olive Shaw's stylish dust jacket and cover design were retained for both the two new volumes.

Poucher said in his preface to the first volume:

> The very favourable reception given to the first edition of this work has been gratifying and has demonstrated the necessity for such a book, dealing with the modern aspects of perfumery.
>
> The opportunity afforded by the early demand for a new edition has been of advantage, enabling the author to effect a thorough revision of the entire book. The varieties, sources, and properties of the more important raw materials are included in the first volume, and in many cases formulae have been given to illustrate their use.

In his preface to the second volume, Poucher explained that it was devoted mainly to the use of substances in the production of the finished article for presentation to the buyer. It also contained a brief but fascinating sketch on the part played by perfumes in history, monographs on natural and artificial flower perfumes, and chapters devoted to soap and tobacco.

The second edition was again generally warmly welcomed, especially in seems in America, where Poucher was fast gaining a great reputation. His old friend Professor Curt Wimmer again congratulated Poucher in his review in the *American Perfumer and Essential Oil Review*. 'He has made a good book better. We are confident that the four thousand copies of this edition will not remain long on the publisher's shelves. Perfume and cosmetic manufacturers know a good thing when they see it. Our advice to them is: Buy this latest Poucher, for you cannot afford to be without it.'

However, one of the very few less than fulsome reviews appeared in the March 1926 issue of *British Soap Manufacturer*. The reviewer, only identified by the initials F.B.G., claimed that too much had been attempted in the provision of information, especially in the chapters on soap, perfumery and tobacco flavours and 'there is much matter of a descriptive nature that might well have been omitted or greatly reduced without detracting from the value of the book'.

Obviously using his experience as a photographer, Poucher had suggested in the book the use of cleaned celluloid cinema films as an enamel for the nails, but the reviewer claimed that with the availability of a great range of celluloid varnishes, this did not seem to be an economic nor practical suggestion. 'Similar criticsm could not doubt be applied to other formula [*sic*] suggested, and this section of the work might well be revised in a future edition, as this does not add to the dignity or value of the book as a serious contribution to the science of modern perfumery, but rather savours of the "Recipe Book", which may be picked up on the bookstalls for a few shillings or even pence.'

The following year, no doubt much to the chagrin of F.B.G., Poucher produced an even more popular monograph on cosmetics, specifically aimed this time not at his fellow professionals but at the general public, with the beguiling title *Eve's Beauty Secrets*. The book was again published by Chapman & Hall, whose publicity described the book as '110 dainty pages with decorative border in colour and a number of charming illustrations'. These were again by Olive Shaw, including a cover that showed a lady admiring herself in a mirror with pots of burning incense all around. The book sold for 3s 6d (17½ p).

Once again, the critics were virtually unanimous in their praise for the little booklet. *Eve* itself said the book was 'more interesting than many novels' and congratulated Poucher for treating a serious subject seriously. 'Not for him any kind of powder, put on any old way; plus any kind of rouge, a lipstick of any bright colour and kohl dabbed on the eyes for a lauguishing effect. He takes us slowly through all the processes of face adornment.'

The *Nottingham Journal* greatly welcomed the book, and concluded: 'It is probable that Milady will declare this the most useful of Mr Poucher's works,' while even the *Daily Mirror* gave a rather backhanded complimentary review of the book. 'Phillida' admitted that she had no idea that 'scent buying' was an art which required such careful study. 'According to this book, blondes and light brunettes must be careful to find the special scents that "blend in with their charms," and we preferred ones are restricted to the use of rose, lilac, lily and violet perfumes, and must avoid those that have a strong and Oriental type of odour.'

The trade press was equally effusive. The *Pharmaceutical Journal*, in what was then a male-dominated industry, said the book would be read with interest by every woman who obtained a copy. 'The mere man even [*sic*] will find much in it that is not only entertaining but instructive. The pharmacist especially – not as a man but as a pharmacist – should certainly be in possession of the book if he does much in supplying the ladies with toilet articles.' The *American Perfumer* sought to score a political point in its review. 'Copies of this little book should be in the hands of those who at present are seeking to restrict and hamper the toilet preparations industry by the passage of State legislation. A copy on file in the New York City Department of Health for the use of certain officials in their leisure moments would do much to keep them out of mischief.' Other reviews appeared in French, German, Spanish and South African journals.

By this time, Poucher was finding himself described as 'probably the world's foremost expert in perfumery and cosmetics' and was being quoted in journals as diverse as *Tit Bits* ('Peril in the Powder-Puff' – on the dangers of certain cosmetics) and the *Weekly Dispatch* ('Miss 1928 using yet more powder'), to the *Gardeners' Chronicle* (on the extraction of flower perfumes) and the *Soap Trade Review* (on soap perfumes – the start of a regular series

WAP, now the top
Yardley perfumier.

in this journal). He was described as 'an artist in perfumes' in a short piece
in the *Daily Sketch* in 1933. 'He designs perfumes and looks like a doctor.'

He now described himself as a consulting chemist and in 1929 moved his
laboratory to the rather more exclusive address of 76 Woodstock Street, just
off Oxford Street in Central London, which he described as 'a rather old-
fashioned but well-equipped laboratory'.

When the third, revised and enlarged, edition of the second volume of *Perfumes, Cosmetics and Soaps* appeared that year, it was already being referred to as 'the New Poucher' and the *vade mecum* on the subject. It was certainly well established as the standard work of reference, and was to run to four editions within nine years of its first publication. The fifth edition of *Perfumes, Cosmetics and Soaps* appeared in three volumes, the third being devoted to the manufacture of cosmetics, soaps and perfumes. To date the work has run to ten editions, has been translated into seven languages, has sold more than 32,000 copies worldwide and is still in print.

A slight problem arose in 1929 when it was discovered that the author of *The American Soap Makers' Guide*, published by his American publisher, D. Van Nostrand in New York, had failed to acknowledge that two of his chapters had been heavily based on Poucher's *Perfumes, Cosmetics and Soaps* Volume II, but an erratum slip was agreed and everyone seemed happy. *Soap Trade and Perfumery Review* reported that it was 'a pleasant termination of what, in the absence of mutual good-will, might have proved a very unpleasant incident, and both parties are to be congratulated on its amicable conclusion.' One wonders what might have happened in today's overtly litigious climate.

Also at about this time, Poucher was selected to contribute monographs on cosmetics and perfumes to the new edition of the *Encyclopedia Britannica*, and he received an illuminated certificate to mark the fact that he had been entered on the roll as a founder subscriber 'whose appreciation and support of scholarship has facilitated the production of the 14th edition'. Poucher also contributed monographs on the same subjects to *Chamber's Encyclopaedia*.

Then in 1934, in one of the great defining moments in his career, Poucher joined the staff of the top British perfumer, Yardley, in their then new premises at Sackville House, 40 Piccadilly, where he took the position of research chemist and perfumer – and where he was to work with much distinction for the next thirty years of his life.

Yardley of London had a long heritage and were world leaders in their field for many years from the middle of the last century. Founder William Yardley was born in 1756 to a family whose ancestors included a powerful Abbot of Kenilworth in Warwickshire in the fifteenth century. In 1620, a young man called Yardley apparently paid King Charles I a sum of money for the concession to exclusively manufacture lavender-scented soap for the city of London, but the records of this enterprise were lost in the Great Fire of London in 1666.

William Yardley acquired the soap and perfume business by bailing out his heavily indebted son-in-law, William Cleaver, whose father had founded the company in 1770. Apparently he was an ambitious man, and the time was not unpropitious as this was an era of elaborate dress and less-than-habitual personal hygiene, with the subsequent use of much perfume by both men and women.

In 1817, William Yardley was also still trading as a sword-cutter in Bloomsbury, but by his death in 1824, he had set up a separate business, supplying lavender, cosmetics and soap. His younger son Charles (1795–1882) took over the business, then known as Yardley and Statham, and exhibited Old Brown Windsor Soap at the Great Exhibition of 1851, in the Crystal Palace in Hyde Park.

The company expanded quickly and by 1910 had moved to its synonymous central London address at 8 New Bond Street. It became a public limited company in 1920, and when the spirit duty on lavender was removed in 1932, business boomed, the turnover doubled and the factory was extended.

The success story of Yardley is inextricably bound up with the fact that English-grown lavender is reckoned to be the finest in the world, and the essential oil obtained from it fetches the highest price. This was especially true for a company operating in a country in which it had once been described as the national perfume, and Yardley was closely connected with Linn Chilvers' creation of lavender fields around Hunstanton and Heacham and a distillery at Fring in north Norfolk.

The company grew fast on the success of its lavender-based perfumes and lavender toilet water, and later expanded into cosmetics, bath products, male and female fragrances and skin care. Following a temporary decline in the early years of the twentieth century, its fortunes were revived by the two brothers, Thornton and Richard Gardner, who transformed Yardley from a local to a national, and later, a worldwide name.

It had been Thornton Gardner's decision to take on Walter Poucher, the rising young star in the cosmetics world, and it must be ranked as one of the best decisions he ever made. It was Poucher's genius in the creation of cosmetics and fragrances that ordinary, working-class women could afford, which really made the company's name. And it was not just the woman in the street who loved Yardley; even the late Queen Mother is said to have rated their products as her favourite fragrance.

The company finally collapsed in 1998 with reported debts of £126 million, and the still-important brand name of Yardley was eventually bought by the German cosmetics giant Wella in 2000. One wonders what Poucher would have thought of that. In a feature on the demise of Yardley which appeared in the *Independent on Sunday* in 2000, Janet Street-Porter wrote: 'I suppose the story of Yardley . . . is that in our modern world, perfumes that traded on an image of gentility and Englishness have lost their appeal. Without the remarkable Mr Poucher to proselytise their products – "I liked this lippy so much I wore it up a Munroe [*sic*]" – Yardley seems to have lost its way.'

Poucher set to work in his new position at Yardley with his usual energy and efficiency, and his career burgeoned as a result. His arrangement was that he would work for only six months of the year, while he devoted the rest of his time to research and his growing and increasingly successful career as a mountain photographer.

While with Yardley, he is credited with the creation of best-selling brands starting with Freesia in 1931 and Bond Street in 1932, and following with such well-known names as Flair, Lotus, Orchis and Elegance. He also created that distinctive smell which identifies Yardley's soap. In a 'Potted

'Bond Street' . . . provocative as the skilful play of a fronded fan . . . as full of beguilement as your eyes can be when you choose. Yardley Perfume enshrines the many-mooded Eve in you! *Yardley, 33 Old Bond Street, London W1*

'BOND STREET'
BY
YARDLEY

Personality' profile in the May 1936 *Yardley News* bulletin, Poucher was described as labouring alone in his ultra-modern laboratory on the fifth floor of Sackville House, working out new formulae for new lines. 'His is the brain that evolves the perfumes and their corresponding odours for powder, cosmetics and soap.'

An examination of the beauty business headed 'Secret Tsars of Beauty', and including a rather staccato portrait of Poucher, appeared in the *London Evening News* in March 1936. 'A Special Correspondent Who Knows' described him thus:

> In a laboratory high above Piccadilly works a smiling-faced young man with a broad northern accent [*sic*]. His name is a household word among perfumers in every country. His two-volumed book on perfumery is a standard work – the only one. His opinions pass unchallenged. He knows more about modern perfumes than any living man. His name is Poucher.
>
> He works for one of the oldest perfumery firms in the country. His creations sell all over the world, and particularly in the United States, where his firm operates a company on a vast scale.
>
> His latest creation is shortly to appear. It will make hundreds of thousands of pounds.

Perhaps all this new-found fame and his obvious love of publicity went to his head, because Poucher received a severe ticking off from the company chairman, Thornton Gardner, following an article which appeared in the *Daily Express* on 9 September 1936. In the article, which concerned the Norfolk lavender harvest at Fring, Poucher was described as being 'the foremost consultant chemist in Britain'.

Poucher, who had spent a fortnight in Norfolk conducting tests for Yardley on the new crop, was quoted as saying: 'Almost all the lavender oil used in Britain comes from France, where the lavender grows wild on the Riviera. But there is no oil, though, to compare with that extracted from the best English lavender. With the gradual development which is going on here Norfolk lavender oil should become world famous.'

In an angry copy letter sent to Poucher at Glenbrittle House on the Isle of Skye, where he was staying on one of his motoring and photographic tours, Gardner said he took 'great exception' to the article.

> I cannot imagine anything more damaging to the British perfumery industry and this business in particular, than the paragraph 'Almost all the lavender [oil] used in Britain comes from France.'
>
> I must point out that [Poucher] is not at present the foremost consultant chemist, but a chemist in the employ of Yardley and Company. Although in certain cases the company do not object to individual names being mentioned in articles for publication on matters concerned with the trade, they should always be quoted as Mr _____ of Yardley's, and the subject of the article should be discussed or submitted to the directors, which principle the directors apply to themselves.

It sounds very much like a case of Yardley's thought police at work, and there could also perhaps have been a hint of jealousy that this new young whippersnapper recruit was grabbing too many headlines for himself, while not mentioning the name of his employers. There was also perhaps the more significant fact that Poucher had been introduced to Queen Mary, grandmother of the present Queen, who was paying a visit to the harvest and distillery at Fring, presumably while staying at nearby Sandringham, while the other directors all seem to have been back in Piccadilly. No wonder the Yardley directors were fuming, because there can be no doubt that they would have felt that *they* should have been the ones introduced to Royalty, not the upstart Poucher.

We are lucky to have a detailed, and indeed unique, insight into Poucher's life at Yardley in another interview in the *Evening News* by Sheila O'Callaghan, who went to see him at work in his top floor laboratory in Piccadilly in January 1938.

The room was charged with the heavy fumes of hundreds of concentrated odours, and my first impression was that Mr Poucher would look equally at home surrounded, not by perfume bottles, but by brief boxes, drafts, deeds, with a judicial wig on his head, a stethoscope hanging round his neck, or a pair of forceps in one hand.

When O'Callaghan hinted at the apparent lack of sympathy between his appearance and his work, Poucher rather disdainfully remarked that he had to take his outwardly prosaic work of concocting smells to turn the head of his fellow man completely objectively, otherwise it would 'get him down'.

'To me it is just chemistry, mathematics, headaches and patience,' he remarked. 'See this locker?' he went on, opening the door of a narrow steel cupboard. 'It's where I keep my outdoor clothes. I always change as well as putting on a white coat on coming in here. If ever I spill anything on my clothes I send them to the cleaner at once – couldn't bear to go out with a smell on me.'

Around the walls of 'Mr Poucher's pungent perfumery', O'Callaghan noted tiers of metal shelves holding bottles of all shapes and sizes, some no bigger than a thimble. Poucher explained that these were the raw materials from all around the world which provided the additional 'notes' (which must have been a pleasing musical analogy for him) from which the perfumes were gradually constructed. When he started in the business, he said, the natural flower extracts and animal tinctures would have filled just a few shelves, but the advent of synthetic chemicals had more than doubled the range.

The journalist was invited to have a whiff of some of these raw materials, which ranged from 'tingling and dusty' to 'something like a dark, damp cellar'. A four-year-old, £10-an-ounce, undiluted tincture of ambergris – taken from the gut of a sperm whale which had eaten a certain species of cuttlefish found in tropical seas – reminded her of nothing so much as mildewed old books. Tincture of musk had a 'pleasantly warm smell', while neat civet and castoreum were apparently 'not the sort of thing you'd ever want to meet twice'.

On the flat black top of Poucher's desk, O'Callaghan noticed groups of glass-stoppered bottles about half full. These were experimental perfumes, he explained. 'You may – or may not – be meeting some of them out in the world one of these days . . . [but] many get scrapped.' Then O'Callaghan spotted what appeared to be surrealist table ornaments – wire stands consisting of a central stem with branches on either side with strips of white paper waving in the breeze from them. She was told that these were the test strips of absorbent paper which the perfumer used to dab on a drop of some tincture or other to have a sniff of a particular scent.

As the heading on the article announced, 'The Nose Has It!', but Poucher told her that such work had to be limited, and that concentration with the nose for longer than two or three hours a day without a break was 'unwise'. Apparently, as he told Andy MacFarlane in Toronto in 1957, violets were the worst offenders. After an hour's work on violets, 'intense olfactic fatigue' set in, and the professional nose forgot every smell it had ever learned – except, that is, for violets.

Finally, Poucher briefly described the mysteries of the process in the making of a new perfume:

> I choose two smells for a base. For perfumery purposes there are only nine different combinations of these two smells. My object is to find the perfect blend – in which neither smell predominates. When I've got it, I proceed to build up the perfume from twenty, thirty or fifty other materials, blending them all the time so that no one predominates over another, or over the particular odour I want to bring out.
>
> Exact measurement of the minutest quantities is necessary, otherwise a gallon of the perfume made at the factory will not smell the same as an ounce made in the laboratory.

CHEMICAL AND ENGINEERING NEWS

That formidable Poucher nose tests perfume from a test strip in his Yardley lab.

He said a perfume could take minutes, days, or years to make. And ideas for a new fragrance could come from anywhere at any time. He described how one of his most successful and quickly attained fragrances had come while he was out playing golf on his beloved Walton Heath course in Surrey. He had suddenly smelt a 'wonderful odour' but, for the life of him, couldn't tell where it came from. His caddie suggested it might have been the avenue of lime trees at the entrance to the club up on the hill. Driving home through that avenue later the same day, Poucher caught that same, overpoweringly strong smell. Next day back in his laboratory, he immediately set to work making up a lime perfume. He returned to the golf course after work on the two following evenings to compare his results with the reality, and then finished off preparing the new lime-based perfume the next day. 'But I'm seldom as lucky as that,' he admitted. Often, he was haunted for months by the remembrance of a wildflower fragrance he could just not place and therefore replicate in a perfume.

O'Callaghan concluded that the modern perfumer had to be both a scientist and an artist. But Poucher may not have agreed with her next remark: 'Some may cultivate an "artistic temperament"; not Mr Poucher. He dispenses with "frills".'

The outbreak of the Second World War in 1939 had a significant effect on Poucher's work as a cosmetic chemist at Yardley, especially when the sources of the more exotic raw materials were blocked and more local materials had to be sourced. When the *Evening Standard* reporter visited Poucher's Piccadilly laboratory in January 1941 to write a story on British perfumes and cosmetics being part of the Board of Trade's campaign to build up Britain's wartime dollar balance, he was described as 'the man creating the new bouquets'. 'He provides a strongly masculine contrast to the samples of delicate, feminine perfumes which surround him. Mr Poucher is a big, loose-limbed man with a quiet speaking voice and a hearty laugh.'

Following up this story a week later, the *Daily Sketch* published a series of action photographs showing Poucher testing perfumes and odours with the paper testing strips, in a wine glass and test tube. The accompanying article claimed that London was fast replacing Paris as a perfumery trade centre, a remark which would have delighted Poucher, who was always very keen to upstage his French rivals.

Research chemists, having in mind the very large range of aromatic plant products grown in the British Empire, have for years been experimenting in anticipation of possible cutting off of certain costly essences and ottos from European countries now under Nazi domination.

At a West End laboratory of a famous perfumery firm (Yardley), familiar domestic smells, such as carrot and celery, vie with the more exotic vegetable and animal extracts, such as patchouli and ambergris, and play their part in the creation of a sophisticated perfume such as Bond Street, which is having a great vogue in overseas markets.

Poucher always seemed to ready with a quote and be able to catch the attention of the press with a 'newsy' line or angle on a story, a habit which, as we have seen, sometimes got him into trouble. One of his often expressed opinions from the 1930s onwards and which always attracted journalists' attention was that it was not only women who should wear make-up and perfume – but men should as well, as he did himself. It does not sound too shocking today, when £632 million is spent annually on male skin care, but at the time, the closest most men would get to this sort of thing would be slightly scented hair cream. These were the days of the Brylcreem Boys, when sports stars like the England football and cricket captains Johnny Haynes and Denis Compton would advertise the stuff, and men would liberally plaster it over their hair.

But Poucher, as always, was prepared to take one step further and, as Ralph Champion rather sensationally reported in the *Daily Mirror* in April 1956, 'In a few years, we men are going to be a bunch of stinkers!' His authority was Poucher – who in typically slipshod tabloid fashion he incorrectly dubbed 'Bill'. Poucher told him that millions of American men were already using scent disguised as hair cream, shaving lotion, talcum powder and after-bath deodorants. 'Bill believes and I agree,' wrote Champion, 'there is nothing cissy in all this.' What was the best masculine odour? Poucher advised: 'Something nice, clean, fresh, sweet and pleasant – but not obtrusive.'

Champion had undoubtedly picked up the story from an interview Poucher had done with United Press staff writer H.D. Quigg in the *New York World Telegram and Sun* on one of his American visits a month before. In this he said: 'Men are getting bolder and bolder – simply because they are getting more conscious of their appearance. The perfume and cosmetic business is going to swing more towards the males. The

Poucher tests perfume from a test strip in his garden.

female is already covered with every type of perfume and cosmetic that can be invented.'

He said that men, especially in America, were already using scent in hair lotions, colognes, shaving cream and other toiletries, such as after shave talc. 'If you call it face powder, no man would buy it – it's a psychological thing,' he said. A year before in an ABC radio interview with Ted Malone, who described him as 'a big, handsome, tweedy Briton with the muscles of a seasoned mountain climber', Poucher had said: 'Half the men on Fifth Avenue are wearing perfume right this minute. We don't call it perfume – if we did they wouldn't touch it – so we call it after-shave lotion, and they use gallons of it.'

In an appreciation of the work of Poucher published on his retirement in the *Perfumery and Essential Oil Record* of December 1959, an editorial by W.R. Littlejohn paid tribute to his prophetic wisdom on the subject of men's cosmetics. 'For many years, and almost playing a lone hand, he forecast the advent of cosmetics for men. Today the volume of business that is being done in this rapidly growing field is evidence once again of his shrewdness and foresight.'

Interviewed by Frank Haley in *Chemist and Druggist* in November 1961, he said he counted as one of his 'failures' being one of the first chemists to adumbrate the use of cosmetics for men five or ten years previously, 'but in 1930 (when I first suggested it) I was told I was mad! Yet look at the sales of such merchandise today, and it is only beginning.'

Robert Calkin, who worked with Poucher as a perfumer for two years after joining Yardley in 1958, told me about his first meeting with 'WAP' – as he was known in those days.

> My first glimpse of the great man was while I was doing my apprenticeship at the Yardley soap factory at Stratford in the East End of London. He arrived in a wide-brimmed, Cecil Beaton type hat, a Saville Row suit and pale blue silk gloves. Whether or not these were appropriate for such a venue was immaterial; WAP never compromised.
>
> He was always true to himself and his belief in the importance of style, quality and 'kudos' (a word which he often used). He frequently wore cosmetics believing that men had just as much right to look 'a million dollars' as women. He seemed impervious to the comments this might elicit.

Calkin said he found the Gardners were delightful people to work for, although he remembered Poucher describing them as 'a bit parsimonious'. By all accounts, however, he was well rewarded for his contribution to the success of the company, and the perfumers – Poucher, Jim Hackforth-Jones, Calkin and later Peter Ellis – enjoyed something of a privileged existence.

During his second, and Poucher's final, year at Yardley, Calkin accompanied him to Geneva to visit Firmenich, one of the leading manufacturers of high-class synthetic materials, and then to Grasse, the home of *parfum* in the south of France, on the annual buying trip. 'In those days,' he recalled, 'Yardley was a very important customer for high-quality perfumery raw materials, such as rose, jasmine, orange blossom and, of course, lavender, and the yearly visit to suppliers was something of a royal progress.' With an order book worth many thousands of pounds, Poucher would visit five or six of the major producers of raw materials in Grasse, taking back samples from the current year's crop to his hotel. At the end of the week orders were placed with the successful suppliers.

'The week was taken up with wining and dining at the best restaurants that Switzerland and the south of France could offer, as the perfumery industry was very rich in those days and much entertaining took place,' said Calkin. 'WAP loved his food, though he never drank alcohol.' The company treated its perfumers very well on such visits and Calkin recalled that in Geneva they always stayed at five-star hotels such as the famous Richmonde Hotel and in Cannes at either the Majestic or the Carlton, where Poucher's wife Dorothy, 'a colourful and interesting lady who shared her husband's love of classical music', had joined them on Calkin's first visit.

> This was a whole new world to me, but WAP made sure I knew what was expected, was always considerate, and he even bought me a suitable tie to replace my own rather conservative choice. Most of the perfumery supply companies were family owned in those days and WAP was always entertained and mixed at the highest level.

Mention has already been made of Poucher's fame across the Atlantic, and he had made several visits before, on 9 December 1954, he became the first Englishman and first perfumer to be awarded the International Gold Medal of the American Society of Cosmetic Chemists. It was also the first time that the award had been made outside America and was given 'for outstanding technical achievement and service to the industry'. The award was made at a glittering ceremony following a Thanksgiving-style banquet (including roast Vermont turkey and cranberry sauce) at the society's annual meeting, held at one of the largest hotels in New York, the Biltmore. The distinguished dinner-jacketed audience included most of the leading chemists, scientists and presidents of companies in the industry in America.

The award was presented by the president-elect of the society, Dr Kenneth L. Russell of the Colgate-Palmolive Company, who told Poucher the award had been made 'in acknowledgment of your outstanding contributions to the science of fragrance and perfume – in recognition of your pioneering efforts in transforming an art to a science, and in appreciation of your exploration in resolute English style of a field shrouded with the cobwebs of mystery.'

Citations were also delivered by Mr Pierre Bouillet of Givaudan-Delawanna Inc., on 'William A. Poucher, The Pioneer' and by Mr H. Gregory Thomas, president of Chanel Inc. on 'William A. Poucher, The

On his frequent visits to the States, WAP (second right at table) was feted everywhere he went by the American perfume industry. This photograph was taken at Lou Walter's exclusive Latin Quarter restaurant in New York.

Man'. Poucher himself responded with an address on 'Ventures into Fragrance', in which he identified perfumery as one of the three arts – alongside music and painting – and the most intangible and least understood of the three. One wonders why, in view of his contemporary fame and acknowledged mastery of the subject, he did not also consider photography and in particular, landscape photography, as perhaps the fourth.

In a paper entitled 'A Classification of Odours and Its Uses', Poucher also used this illustrious occasion to unveil his revolutionary idea for the numerical classification of the strength of the odours of raw materials used in perfumery. Following four years research on the subject, he proposed that they should be classified on the basis of the length of time they evaporated at a laboratory temperature of 16°C. Admitting that this method depended 'upon the reliability of the nose', Poucher said that odours of the longest duration were given a coefficient of 100, whereas those that evaporated in less than a day had a reading of one. Thus long-lasting fragrances such as patchouly and oakmoss rated 100, and so on down the scale. Using a familiar musical analogy, he rated substances with a coefficient of 1–14 'top notes', 15–60 'middle notes' and 61–100 'basic notes' or 'fixers'. Thus Poucher's perfume Flair, which he developed in 1957, is said to have a soft citrus top note and a chypre (a scent from from Cyprus) musky bottom note. Robert Calkin said that this system was now universally accepted, with some modification, by all perfumers today. 'To repeat WAP's experiment remains one of the basics in the training of young perfumers.'

The American award put the seal on a brilliant career in cosmetics, and reports of Poucher's success were carried by all the trade press back home. While in New York, he was interviewed by Dave Garroway on his NBC TV early morning show *Today*, which had an estimated audience of three million, and conducted a bouquet test using jasmine and lavender essences live in front of the cameras. *Soap, Perfumery and Cosmetics* magazine reckoned those seven minutes of coverage were worth £10,000 in free advertising for the British perfume industry.

In another interview by Edyth Thornton McLeod, which was syndicated to about 100 newspapers across America, Poucher said that perfume should be worn as part of a woman's dress, just like their undergarments. 'Look here,' he said, 'tell your women just to pour the perfume down the front of their dresses, don't just dab a piece of cotton with a few drops!' One can imagine that the Yardley bosses would have been delighted with the possible sales that might have resulted from that piece of advice.

Fifteen months later, the American Society of Perfumers awarded Poucher an honorary membership at its second annual symposium at Essex House, New York, and he was again fêted by his American friends. Also during this visit, he was interviewed by Ted Malone for ABC radio, a programme that was carried by over 275 stations across the country.

Poucher left a surprisingly modern impression of the cosmetic enhancement of American women ('No one asked me about the men – their ties are just too marvellous') after his New York visits. In a subsequent *Yardley News* article he wrote:

> Go into the lounge of any luxury hotel about tea-time and there you will see the smart New Yorkers. They are elegantly and expensively dressed in model gowns, partially hidden by mink; but look carefully at their faces, and through the heavy façade of cosmetics you may see, if you have a discerning eye, those tell-tale signs of face-lifting which are supposed to take ten years off anyone's appearance.
>
> Then sally forth into 5th Avenue on Easter Day, and see the Parade; and what a contrast: for here you will encounter the real belles of New York, decked in gay dresses and coats of many colours. Nylons and new shoes are worn by all and sundry, and their beautifully made-up faces are crowned by the most provoking flowered bonnets. If you have ever been in Paris you will search in vain for the invisible halo which characterises the women of France, but here in New York you will be lucky if you can smell the faintest whiff of perfume!

WAP, pictured at his desk at Yardley's.

Soap, Perfumery and Cosmetics had paid one of the most glowing tributes that Poucher received on his Gold Medal award: 'In so far as genius is an infinite capacity for taking pains, WAP is not far removed from being a cosmetological and perfumery genius. Watching him at work, one notes with something approaching awe the meticulous care with which he narrows down possibilities to probabilities and probabilities to certainties.'

In 1956 he received the award of honorary membership of the American Society of Perfumers, 'in recognition of his distinctive service to the Perfumery and Cosmetic Industry'. He had been made the first honorary member of the Society of Cosmetic Chemists of Great Britain at only its fourth annual meeting, and by now he was also a Fellow of the Pharmacuetical Society, in addition to his Fellowship of the Royal Photographic Society.

Poucher retired from Yardley at the age of sixty-nine after thirty years service in December 1959, when an informal dinner was held in his honour at the Mirabelle Restaurant in London. The menu was appropriately divided into Vol. I, Vol. II and Vol. III courses, in reference to Poucher's classic work *Perfumes, Cosmetics and Soaps*, and was printed in Latin.

At another farewell luncheon also held at the Mirabelle a week later, the Yardley chairman Mr Lyddon Gardner recalled it was Poucher who had created the Bond Street perfume – 'the only English perfume of international reputation and the best perfume that has ever borne the name of Yardley'. He added:

> Bond Street is unique in being created by an Englishman and being sold throughout the world by an English house. The very high reputation which the name Yardley carries for perfumed toilet articles is a result of his constant and successful work in this field (of the creation of perfumed products), his name is the terror of Grasse (Yardley's most important source of raw materials in the south of France). It is known that Poucher will not accept anything for Yardley that is not of top quality and priced at a fair figure. However, this terror which he inspires is tempered with respect for his art and knowledge and affection for his personality and character.

Perhaps in preparation for and recognition of the next brilliantly successful chapter in his life, he was presented with a new, state-of-the-art Leica camera as his retirement gift. Robert Calkin recalls: 'There were a few

raised eyebrows that Poucher had asked to be given the camera in question, which was the most expensive around. But then Poucher, who was a perfectionist in all things, would have been happy with nothing less.'

In another tribute published in *Perfumery and Essential Oil Record* that month, it was stated: 'In all fields of human endeavour from time to time there emerges a figure who makes his mark indelibly upon his chosen field and one who leaves a lasting impression in the record books. In the perfumery field W.A. Poucher is such a man.'

5. A CAMERA IN THE HILLS

Walter Poucher first visited his beloved Lake District shortly before he joined up for the Army in 1912, and he had another excursion to the Lakeland fells while on leave from the RAMC around 1914.

It was always a very special place for him, and he was to end his days peacefully there in 1988, in the Thornthwaite nursing home on the shores of Bassenthwaite Lake, overlooking Skiddaw and the northern Lakeland fells. When he died, his ashes were scattered just across the Whinlatter Pass on Low Fell, near Loweswater.

As he describes in the preface of his first mountain photography book, *Lakeland Through the Lens*, published by Chapman & Hall at 18s (65p) while Britain was in the midst of wartime uncertainty in 1940, he was intent on proving that it was possible to take successful photographs of the hills despite the notorious Lakeland weather.

OPPOSITE: Poucher, Leica round his neck, in his favoured environment.

BELOW: Poucher on the ice-rimed summit of Glyder Fawr in 1941.

> In my early days, I experienced many of the disappointments associated with mountain photography, and some years ago at Wasdale, I was not encouraged to hear a photographer express the view that really successful pictures of the Lakeland landscape were impossible owing to its affinity for the moisture-laden atmosphere of the Atlantic.

This was apparently a commonly-held view at the time, but Poucher claimed with typical bravado that his first book was 'the complete answer to any such conception which may still be entertained'. One who held these views was apparently his great contemporary and rival in the field of mountain photography, Frank Smythe. Poucher told his son John that he had heard Smythe say in a lecture at a Fell & Rock Climbing Club dinner that he doubted if a book of photographs devoted entirely to the Lake District hills was possible, due to the prevailing bad weather. Poucher obviously set out to prove him wrong, and the book was dedicated to his fellow members of the club.

The book took the form of a walking tour through the district, starting from Mardale (interestingly just before Manchester Corporation flooded the valley to form the present Haweswater reservoir) and High Street, to Helvellyn, Saddleback (as Blencathra was commonly known then), Derwentwater, Borrowdale, Great End and Esk Hause, Sty Head and Lingmell, Honister and Buttermere, Ennerdale, Wastwater, Pillar, Great Gable, Scafell, Eskdale, Langdale, Crinkle Crags and Bowfell, and ending up on the Coniston Fells.

What a wonderful walking tour that was, and would still be today. Poucher's son John appears in the foreground of many of the photographs in the book, but these must have been taken some years before, as John at the time was at stationed at Prestatyn, training for his own Army service. Typical is the shot looking down on Watendlath from the pony track which leads up from the hamlet to Rosthwaite in Borrowdale. Wearing his favourite black cap, the young John sits rather disconsolately, arms on knees, on a broken-down dry-stone wall gazing down on the little Norse settlement made famous as the home of Judith Paris by Hugh Walpole in his *Rogue Herries* novels. 'I would often have to wait like that for what seemed like ages for the light to come exactly right for father,' he told me.

The book came about as a result of the interest which Chapman & Hall's director, E.W. Hamilton, had shown in Poucher's mountain photography. Of course, Chapman & Hall had been the publishers of his classic works on perfumery, and, knowing that Hamilton was a great lover of the hills himself, Poucher decided to approach them first. *Lakeland through the Lens* was well received, and Chapman & Hall went on to publish another twelve of Poucher's large-format photographic books.

ABOVE: Mardale before the coming of the reservoir.

RIGHT: Watlendlath, featuring John Poucher.

A Camera in the Hills

Two of the most interesting reviews of that first book came from Frank Smythe himself, who had apparently previously claimed that such a book was not possible. He wrote in the *Observer* in October 1940: 'In technique Mr Poucher's work is first rate. In artistic sense he has still something to learn. There is a certain conventionality about his composition which consist mainly of middle distance and long range landscapes.' He continued:

> His own criticism of Plate no 11 (a hazy May shot of Wasdale from the climbers' track to Scafell) implies a lack of appreciation of atmospheric quality. Also, while he reproduces clouds faithfully, he does not appear to realise their immense importance in mountain scenes, otherwise he would have tried to capture those difficult, elusive, and beautiful vistas of sunshine, cloud, and storm that in the British hills are worth more of beauty than a hundred sunny days.

And his view of the photograph of a party of four walkers crossing the footbridge near Burnthwaite in Wasdale en route to Great Gable, which towers in the background, managed to be both topical and scathing. It was, he wrote, 'an example of a good picture spoilt by the inclusion of human figures, apparently some of the Hitler Youth goose-stepping'.

But in the *Alpine Journal* of May 1941, Smythe must have eaten his words, because he paid this glowing tribute: 'With every respect to the mountaineers and photographers who toiled up the hills in years gone by with large cameras and loads of plates, and made the hills of the country live for us in books, calendars and postcards, this book undoubtedly contains the finest collection of photographs of Lakeland ever published in one book.' The *Illustrated London News* agreed: 'What Mr Smythe has done for Mont Blanc and its fellows in his Alpine album has been done for this more familiar region in a similar volume, charmingly pictured and annotated with practical conciseness.'

Smythe's comment about cameras was a reference to the fact that Poucher had made extensive use of what was then known as a 'miniature'

Footbridge below
Great Gable.

camera (what today would be called a 35mm) instead of the bulky and very heavy wooden glass plate cameras used in the past by people like George and Ashley, the renowned Abraham brothers of Keswick. As Poucher explained in the comprehensive photographic notes in the book, he mainly used his Leica IIIA 'miniature' and occasionally his Etui 3½ x 2½in, which could be adapted for film packs, roll film and plates and folded down like a miniature.

In an interview by Frank Haley, which appeared in *Cumbria* magazine in December 1961, Poucher paid tribute to his predecessors, and the difficulties they faced compared to those he faced himself.

I came along after them (the Abrahams), inspired by what they had shown everybody. Remember they pioneered routes, then added to their difficulties – and dangers – by humping heavy materials with them. It was a four-man job, one to carry the heavy camera and plates, one the stand (tripod), one the food and one the mountaineering gear. They were restricted on what they could take because of the

Esk Dale head from Hardknott.

small number of plates, unlike the man with a miniature camera, with 36 shots in it and several more casettes in his bag. The Abrahams contributed a tremendous amount to mountain photography, and they were forced to do it the hard way.

No less a luminary than Monica Dickens had made *Lakeland Through the Lens* her Book of the Week in the Manchester *Sunday Chronicle* published at the height of the Battle of Britain in September, 1940. 'It shows in story and picture the majestic [*sic*] of beauties of the English Lake District, so remote from war, and yet so symbolical of the England that all the noise of war is about,' she wrote. 'This is a book to treasure and keep. Turn these pages and you will find the beauty that no war can scar and the peace which is eternal.'

Lakeland Through the Lens was followed in fairly short order by *Snowdonia through the Lens* (1941, dedicated to his photographer friend Gerald Lacey), *Lakeland Holiday* (1942, dedicated to his son John, then serving in the Army), *Snowdon Holiday* (1943, dedicated to the distinguished

climber Geoffrey Winthrop Young) and *Scotland through the Lens* (1943, dedicated to his wife Dorothy), all published and printed in photogravure by Chapman & Hall in the same large format. All took the form of illustrated descriptions of walking tours through the respective areas, with son John often providing the human interest in the foreground of shots. Each book too had a table of photographic data at the conclusion, telling the reader which camera and lens were used for each shot, the exposure, the aperture and whether a filter was used.

While *Snowdonia through the Lens* covered the most popular and better-known peaks of North Wales, *Snowdon Holiday* was the photographic description of a May holiday Poucher spent exploring the then little-known and more out of the way places like Craig-yr-Ysfa, the Black Ladders and Cwm Glas, the Moelwyns and Cnicht. There is also a full account of a traverse of the famous Snowdon Horseshoe, which he says he walked no less than three times for the purpose of getting the photographs for the book.

Lakeland Holiday is notable because it shows the flooding of Mardale by the encroaching Haweswater reservoir, following the recent completion of the Haweswater Dam by Manchester Corporation. There are shots of

A Camera in the Hills

dry-stone-walled roads disappearing under the rising waters, and the dismantled remains of the seventeenth-century Mardale Church, now also lost to view. There is also a rare example of Poucher's sense of humour, expressed in a charming photograph headed 'Caught Trespassing' of a small black Herdwick lamb stuck between the bars of a gate labelled 'Private' near Overbeck in Wasdale, and looking back helplessly towards the camera. Poucher explained how he and a friend had released the lamb, and added: 'The picture is perhaps unusual for a book of this sort, but it is amusing, and maybe unique.'

The same walking tour format was adopted for *Lakeland Journey* and *Highland Holiday* (both 1945), *Peak Panorama* (1946), *A Camera in the Cairngorms* (1947) and *Over Lakeland Fells* (1948). *Lakeland Journey* was a disappointment to Poucher, because he had hoped to secure a series of pristine snowy pictures of the Lakeland landscape, but he admits he chose the wrong winter, and was faced with spring-like weather with high temperatures and much rain. He would be equally disappointed today, when the effects of global warming mean that the Lakeland hills are seldom snow-covered for very long.

LEFT: Disappearing road, Mardale.

RIGHT: Deepdale.

In his introduction to this book, Poucher describes what to him is the ideal mountain inn, citing the Wastwater Hotel in Wasdale, the Clachaig Inn in Glencoe and the Pen-y-Pass Hotel on the Llanberis Pass in Snowdonia as three of the best. And on the subject of food, a matter always very close to Poucher's heart, he sounded a warning note about one unnamed hotel which had obviously offended his sensitive olfactory feelings:

> There are doubtless many who hold the view that food is the most important item at any hotel, and in remote districts it is a great advantage if a farm is part of the organisation, for there is nothing better than fresh farm produce. While this may be true enough when the food is perfectly cooked in a clean kitchen, I have unpleasant memories of the revolting odour of mutton which used to permeate one hotel, and I always found it detracted considerably from the gastronomic pleasures anticipated after a long day out on the hills.

A Camera in the Hills

Grindsbrook from
Ringing Roger.

An unusual feature of *Lakeland Journey* was the inclusion at the end of the book of a picture quiz asking the readers to test their knowledge of the fells by identifying the sites of eleven Lakeland cairns. We don't know how many took up the challenge, but it may not have been many because no prize was apparently offered. This novel experiment in reader participation was never repeated, and in any case, readers could get the answers by writing to Chapman & Hall.

Peak Panorama, published in 1946 and dedicated to his publisher, John Bale, was Poucher's first excursion into the Pennines, and provides a wonderful time capsule of the area as it was when the campaign to make it Britain's first National Park was at its height. There are memorable photographs of a steam train puffing across the Monsal Dale viaduct (the Midland line closed in 1968 and is now the Monsal Trail walking and riding route), and the railway lines of the Cromford and High Peak Railway (now the High Peak Trail) are still in place beneath the eponymous Railway Slab at Cromford Black Rocks.

Monsal Dale Viaduct.

Poucher stayed at the Church Hotel, Edale (now the Ramblers' Inn), where mine host was the legendary Fred Heardman, a great access and National Park campaigner who also owned the nearby Nag's Head Hotel, and who gained the nickname among local gamekeepers of 'Bloody Bill the Bogtrotter' when he regularly trespassed on Kinder Scout. Poucher describes his 'sunny smile, soft voice and intimate knowledge of the Peak (which) soon endear him to the hearts of all visitors'. Poucher makes little mention of the access problems which faced walkers wanting to cross the highest point of the Peak District at that time, other than to say that the most attractive expedition on Kinder was the circuit of its edges. 'These are justly famous for the strange variety and amazing structure of the stones displayed, but to see them all involves a walk of about fifteen miles, entirely on preserved ground where the trespasser, if caught, may be prosecuted.'

In his preface, however, Poucher adds his name to those who were pushing for the Peak to become a National Park. 'This would not only

Millstone Edge.

eliminate the risk of trespass, which is one of its present disadvantages, but it would encourage a wider exploration of the district by the youth of Britain in the coming years and so help to build up the health of the Nation.' This view was supported and welcomed by the reviewer 'L.H.' in *Out of Doors* magazine.

A Camera in the Cairngorms, published in 1947 still under wartime economy standards, was of a smaller, 18 x 25cm, format. In his preface, Poucher claims that it was a foregone conclusion that this massive and remote group of hills 'resplendent with many a spectacle of wild grandeur' would ultimately become one of Britain's National Parks. In the event, it was to be almost another sixty years before the Cairngorms National Park was established by the Scottish Assembly. 'As usual,' he rather uncharitably concludes in the preface, 'I have given away all my camera secrets at the end of this work, and from the voluminous correspondence I receive it is evident that amateur photographers continue to profit from my experiences.'

Cornices on Lochnagar.

Lairig Ghru and Poucher.

His first book for Country Life, for whom by now he was starting to contribute the first of what were to be many illustrated articles for their magazine, was *Escape to the Hills,* published in 1943. Poucher's illustrated articles for *Country Life* became regulars in that upper class, quintessentially English journal. As well as covering most of the mountainous areas of England, Wales, Scotland and Ireland, Poucher used its columns to describe his many trips abroad, including the Alps, the Canadian Rockies, and the western states of the USA.

Poucher always claimed to be the first Englishman to have walked in and out of the Grand Canyon – a claim that would be hard to prove or disprove – and he described the trip in a *Country Life* article published in October 1949. After exploring the various viewpoints of the South Rim, he descended by the Kaibab Trail in the company of a Californian, whom he noted that despite the hot sun was not wearing a hat, and a Chinese student, wearing low shoes which quickly filled with sand. Climbing out in eleven hours via the Bright Angel Trail, he accomplished the 20-mile trip in two days, staying overnight in the glorious setting of Phantom Ranch, the only accommodation in the canyon bottom. He described the Grand Canyon as 'one of the wonders of the world', and the strange, upside-down quality of walking down 5,000 feet into the canyon from the 7,000-foot South Rim 'summit', and then up again to the 8,000-foot North Rim.

He described the 'Masterpieces of Nature' represented by the Zion and Bryce Canyon National Parks in an article published in *Country Life* in December 1950. Zion Canyon was, he said, 'perhaps the best-known example of a deep, narrow, vertically-walled, vividly-coloured chasm whose floor carries a road giving access to most of it for easy observation'. All of Poucher's pictures appear to have been taken from the roadside at various points in Zion. Today's visitors are no longer allowed to drive into the canyon but have to take shuttle buses instead.

The incredible eroded pinnacles of Bryce also had a big effect on Poucher, as his marvellous series of photographs show. He walked about a mile into the canyon from Fairyland and visited the various viewpoints, concluding that he had been convinced of its 'superlative scenic qualities, the sheer beauty of the golden hues of which I shall never forget'.

Another of these articles, published in August, 1952, was entitled 'The Most Remote Spot in USA' and covered his visit to Monument Valley on the Utah–Arizona border, which he described as being then 'perhaps the most inaccessible spot in the whole of this vast continent'. He made the 650-mile trip from Salt Lake City not knowing whether the 215-mile track across the desert from the main highway would be passable after heavy rainfall or whether they would be able to obtain petrol in the desert. He eventually reached the amazing, soaring buttes and mesas of Monument Valley, where he met Harry Goulding, who had established the first trading post there twenty-seven years before and had advised the many Hollywood producers (who must have included John Ford for his 1939 classic western *Stagecoach*, starring John Wayne, which used the area as a film backdrop).

In the 7 January issue in 1954 he describes his visit to the spectacular Yosemite National Park in California, illustrated with a stunning series of black and white photographs of the soaring granite monoliths and water-falls from all the main viewpoints. Interestingly, he mentions a visit he made to the studio of Ansel Adams, whom he describes as 'one of America's foremost mountain photographers', but there is no hint that they ever met.

Eight years later, in January 1962, he was describing the 'Wonder Lakes of the (Canadian) Rockies', featuring Lake Louise, Moraine Lake, Peyto Lake, Emerald Lake and Lake O'Hara. He mentions that he had a cousin who had lived in Canada and was a member of the Canadian Alpine Club, who had recommended Lake Louise as a good centre, so Poucher followed his advice and was apparently not disappointed. 'The visitor only has to stand on the steps of the Château Hotel on a sunny summer morning to be held spellbound by the grandeur of the scene as a whole and by the infinite variety of colours.'

His first book for Country Life, *Escape to the Hills*, hit the bookshops at 25s (£1.25) and was reprinted in 1944 and 1945, with a revised edition coming out in 1952. Covering the entirety of the higher British mountain areas, Poucher's photographic essays range from the Lake District through to the Scottish Highlands and finally Snowdonia. In his introduction, Poucher returns a familiar musical analogy in describing 'The Charm of the Hills':

> The music of the hills . . . is one of their charms, for the themes change with the weather. You need not be a climber to hear them, for you may sit by a stream which prattles away on its stony bed, or sings sweet

ABOVE: Rosa Burn, Arran.

RIGHT: Gloom in Borrowdale.

ABOVE: Summit Ridge of Sgorr Dheag.

RIGHT: An Gearanach and Steall Waterfall from Glen Nevis.

songs on the dry days as it slips quietly over the rocks on its way to the lowlands. After rain, instead of the clear notes of the flute, you hear the deep boom of the basses as the torrent plunges over boulders and rushes through narrow ravines on its way to the sea. The wind plays its part in this great orchestra when it screams though the gullies and shrieks over the ridges.

Sydney Spencer gave a favourable review of the book for the *Alpine Journal,* commenting: 'Mr Poucher is evidently a mountaineer of the right type, as climbing for its own sake is not what he seeks, although obviously he must have had to accomplish a considerable amount of strenuous scrambling in the course of his expeditions.' *The Times Literary Supplement* called it 'the most comprehensive collection of his work published so far', while H.W. Greenwood's review in the *Photographic Journal* said: 'Of the photographic quality of the book it suffices to say that it most worthily upholds Mr Poucher's reputation as a master of the miniature camera and consummate artist in mountain photography.

This was followed by his second excursion into the Pennines, this time the result of a six-week walking tour and including the Yorkshire Dales as well as the Peak District. *The Backbone of England* was published in 1946 and reprinted in 1948 and 1951. In this book he devoted a whole section to the long battle for access to mountain and moorland, and to access campaigner Tom Stephenson's proposal for a 250-mile Pennine Way long distance path between Edale in the Peak and Wooler (eventually Kirk Yetholm) in Northumberland. 'It is . . . well known that much of the moorland in the Derbyshire Peak is private ground: the notice boards which acquaint the pedestrian with this unfortunate fact are legion and confront him at almost every turn in the high ground.'

After giving a brief history of the long unsuccessful Parliamentary battle to gain the right to roam on open country, Poucher admitted that there were many who claimed that walkers should stick to the country roads or the mountain tracks that already existed. 'The . . . argument is unsound,' he claims, 'because no real pleasure can be obtained from long road walks owing to motor traffic; moreover such a course completely rules out solitude, a much-prized attribute searched for and treasured by all mountain walkers.'

In the Pennines, says Poucher, the paths were few and far between and covered only a small part of the high ground. 'Anyone who doubts this state of affairs should try to amble on Kinderscout, a bare peaty plateau of some thirteen square miles which is uncrossed by a single right of way. He will be lucky if he is not accosted by a keeper and turned back off the moor.'

He concluded that the realisation of Stephenson's dream would be 'a worthy tribute to those of our fighting men who love the hills, and the many beauty spots of our island heritage'. It would be another nineteen years before Stephenson's 'long green trail' would finally be achieved and become the first official long-distance footpath in Britain.

The Backbone of England is also significant because Poucher's photographs show the last remains of the village of Derwent, which, like Mardale in the Lakes, was about to be inundated by the rising waters of a reservoir. The huge Ladybower Reservoir was officially unveiled by King George VI and Queen Elizabeth soon after Poucher was there in 1945. The spire and much of the walls and interior of the former Victorian parish church of St John and St James are shown in Poucher's historic pictures, and the sad ruins of Derwent Hall, once a shooting lodge for the Dukes of Norfolk and later one of the first youth hostels in the Peak, have the waters of the new reservoir lapping at their foundations. The remains are still sometimes visible in times of drought.

Wanderings in Wales, a south–north journey through the principality published by Country Life in 1949, was dedicated to his walking companions Richard Balcomb, Norman Taylor and Robert Tyssen-Gee. In it, Poucher controversially describes the Welsh people as if they were from a foreign country. 'It is well-known that about half the population is concentrated in the iron and coal bearing valley of Glamorgan, that the

Great Rocks Dale.

Derwent Church.

whole race is hardy, and that they are very musical. In addition, most of them are bi-lingual and prefer to converse among themselves in their own Celtic tongue.'

But in his many visits to the principality, he said he had found the natives friendly, and claimed that the national lack of appreciation of the area might be due to the fact that 'the Welsh scenery as a whole had never been fully disclosed to the traveller, either by publicity or by the camera artist who has perceived its real charm'.

Over Lakeland Fells (Chapman & Hall, 1948) was a departure in that Poucher's suggested route took the form of a continuous, seventeen-day high traverse of the main ridges of the Lake District, starting from Shap and ending at Ambleside. He took most of his photographs for the book during May 1943, when he was blessed with fine weather. The *Lake District Herald* claimed it was one of the most notable of Poucher's attractive books. 'It may not be everyone's pidgin to attempt to walk all the ridges of the Lake District

Pen-y-Gader, Cadair Idris.

A Camera in the Hills

. . . but for those unable to make these heady climbs among primeval rocks and ridges W.A. Poucher . . . has added to the nine volumes he has published since he astonished the photographic world by publishing *Lakeland Through the Lens*.'

Poucher's and many other peoples' favourite book was *The Magic of Skye* published at 30s (£1.50) by Chapman & Hall to great critical acclaim in 1949. This is still the most sought-after of all the Poucher titles, and a copy in good condition, with its dust jacket showing the Cuillins from Elgol (one of Poucher's own personal favourite photographs), can today fetch between £80 and £100.

'Never before . . . has Skye been so beautifully captured,' exclaimed *Country Life*, while *The Scotsman* called it 'a deluxe portfolio of pictures which will enchant alike those who have long been under the spell of the Misty Isle and those who still have to cross the tempting kyles'. Iain Colquhoun, in his rather over-the-top review for the *News Chronicle*, Whiteless Pike.

The Old Man of Storr.

claimed: 'If the world is too much for you, if life has become weary, stale, flat and especially unprofitable, you must certainly go to Skye. If is it utterly impossible for you to go to Skye, you must at once read Mr Poucher's latest book about the place. You will then light out for the Coolins [*sic*] as fast as you can, and be much the better for it.'

The Scotsman reviewer added: 'The scores of photographs have an almost theatrical appeal, so superbly do they catch the kaleidoscope of contour. Mr Poucher has paid his subject matter the compliment of long and careful study under all conditions of light, and he may congratulate himself, experienced photographer of mountains that he is, on setting himself a new standard of accomplishment.' *The Scotsman* also praised Poucher's comprehensive listing of Gaelic names at the front of the book and the endpaper maps by 'E.L.B.'.

James Adams, however, writing in the *Glasgow Herald*, had a problem with Poucher's wilderness imagery.

I wish . . . Mr Poucher could break his attachment to mere emptiness, however beautiful he may find it. Skye's mountains provide the busiest climbing ground we have, but that is not reflected in the book. Even in the plates of Glen Brittle Lodge and Staffin, Mr Poucher seems to have been at pains to use his camera only when no fellow human being would mar his composition.

A book picturing Skye which can contrive completely to omit the Sgianachs [the people of Skye], deliberately neglects what could be one of its rarest assets. I admire Mr Poucher's camera work, but I regret his judgement in seeking to 'depopulate'. For Skye is a fine place to live in, it's a bonny isle to visit, but its real charm lies less in the scenery than in its people.

The bumper 224-page book (almost twice the length of most of the others in the series) includes a scene that Poucher rated among his own personal favourites – the sawtooth ridge of the Cuillins from Gars-bheinn

LEFT: Poucher at the Quiraing.

RIGHT: The Quiraing, from the Prison.

to Sgurr nan Gillean as seen from across the waters of Loch Scavaig at Elgol. 'This view is one of the wonders of Skye and its magic appeals to everyone who is lucky enough to see it,' he wrote.

If you are a mountaineer and familiar with the Coolins, you can pick out all the peaks except those hidden by the great ridge of the Dubhs, and will doubtless recall the many happy days you have spent climbing them. If you are a tourist who loves the mountain landscape, you too will find much to please, for nowhere else in Britain will you see such an array of shapely hills all rising directly from the sea.

A Camera in the Hills

LEFT: Duntulm Castle, Skye.

RIGHT: The Cioch on Sron na Ciche in the Guillins.

Poucher also traversed parts of the famous Cuillin Ridge, a mighty test for all scramblers and perhaps the finest mountain excursion in the whole of Britain. But he appears to have baulked at doing the entire 15-mile, 10–12 hour trip, with its 10,000 feet of ascent and descent and eleven Munros (peaks over 3,000 ft), in one expedition, preferring to accomplish it with his 'Good Companions' in sections.

The Surrey Hills published by Chapman & Hall in 1949 was a departure because it was the first Poucher picture book whose subject was not the uplands. This was his personal love letter to his home territory, where he had lived since 1923, and it was dedicated to James Braid, five times Open winner and fellow member of the Walton Heath Golf Club. In the introduction, he explains how he and his wife had grown to love Surrey's 'dainty

Pinnacle Ridge, Coolins.

Coolins from Elgol.

A Camera in the Hills

First hole, Walton
Heath Golf Club.

silver birches, fine old Scots pines and the masses of rhododendrons that splash the whole neighbourhood with colour in the late spring'. The other attraction was the proximity of the heathery expanses of Walton Heath, where his wife Dorothy could ride and he could enjoy excellent golf on its two first class courses.

No less a reviewer than the well-known landscape photographer J. Allan Cash writing in the *Photographic Journal* claimed to be delighted with the book, but perhaps surprisingly wanted more in the way of text from the author: 'Mr Poucher writes very well and we do not get enough descriptive matter with the pictures. Full use has been made of clouds and good lighting. Mr Poucher once even dropped his golf clubs in the middle of a game in order to photograph the nearby countryside during a sudden and particularly beautiful spell of lighting.'

Cash picked up on a common criticism among photographers about Poucher's work: the excessive use of the orange filter. 'He has used it extensively in the pictures for this book, and it certainly enhances many of them.

Loss of mountain grandeur has been made up for by the delightful contrasts between trees or buildings and the sky above and beyond.' Indeed, some believe that Poucher's *contra jour* snow scenes among the birches and pines of Walton Heath in *The Surrey Hills* compare favourably with the best of Frank Smythe.

The only other lowland book which Poucher was to produce was *West Country Journey*, published by Country Life in 1957. In his introduction he describes the frustrations of the photographer waiting for a windless day to capture the reflections in the harbours of the West Country, only to find that when he got there the tide was out. And he was also frustrated by the notorious sea mists and low clouds of Devon and Cornwall. He had to visit Falmouth and Penzance four times and Land's End five times before he found the lighting conditions to his liking.

He evidently liked the rugged coast of Cornwall better than that of Devon. 'The Cornish seaboard is magnificent throughout its entire length, yielding innumerable subjects for the camera, but the same cannot be said of Devon,' where 'there are few localities that provide really striking material for the composing of outstanding pictures'. It was only the wild tor-topped expanses of Dartmoor that compensated for this lack of photographic subjects, which he said he had particularly met along the southern coastline of the county.

Reviewers, however, loved the book, and the *Southern Daily Echo* praised Poucher's images of 'golden beaches, rugged headlands, quiet estuaries and the bleak and lonely moors. He has succeeded by imaginative techniques in portraying some of their finest and most interesting features.' And the *Bath and Wiltshire Chronicle* called it a 'wonderful pictorial record'.

Lakeland Scrapbook, the last Poucher book to be published by Chapman & Hall, in 1950, broke away from the usual format of a consecutive journey through the area, instead of which it used a thematic treatment, covering eleven topics including hills, crags, dales, lakes, tarns, streams and rivers. Unusually, no complete ascent of a peak is described, as Poucher somewhat immodestly claimed to provide 'the complete *vade*

Hartland Quay cliffs.

mecum of Lakeland for the camera artist'. Poucher was responding to the requests from several correspondents who felt there were aspects of the area that had not been covered in his previous books. Appropriately, he dedicated the book to E.W. Hamilton, the director of Chapman & Hall, whom he described as 'a great lover of these hills and an enthusiastic co-operator in the production of this series'.

J.E.B. Wright, writing in *Mountain Craft* 'as a mountaineer not a photographer', said the book 'gives further proof of the dramatic quality of Mr Poucher's mountain photography; through his camera even the trees in winter take on a beauty and grandeur which is not diminished by the hills in the background.' And he noted the better reproduction being achieved by the use of larger photographic plates by the publisher from Poucher's tiny negatives.

I have looked again at all the Poucher books and made yet another wonderful journey through 1,500 photographs of the hills of the Lake

LEFT: Bideford.

RIGHT: Riders at Hound Tor.

District, North Wales, Scotland, the Pennines, Surrey and Derbyshire. Improvements in reproduction in the later books are very marked, some plates measuring 16 x 12in compared with the modest 6 x 4in of my favourite Great Gable photograph.

W.E. Ball wrote in *The Photographic Journal*: 'The photographs themselves are stirring, of excellent quality and well produced. . . . It would appear that Mr Poucher seldom produces a picture that has not the right lighting.

Poucher's first overseas excursion into print came with *The Magic of the Dolomites,* published by Country Life in 1951, a collection which many admirers rate next to *The Magic of Skye* in terms of picture quality. The book was the result of a three-month visit Poucher paid with his wife, during which he drove most of the roads and passes of this delectable corner of northern Italy and climbed several of its famous peaks by the 'tourist' routes, ending in a tremendous thunderstorm on the Bocco di Brenta.

Bowerman's Nose.

In his introductory notes, Poucher delves into the origin of the mountains and credits the rather surprising source of Baron Richthofen for the theory that they were the result of 'animal activity'. This is not quite as outrageous as its sounds, because the magnesium limestone that forms the Dolomites was originally laid down as the remains of sea creatures and corals in a semi-tropical Carboniferous sea.

It certainly surprised the *British Journal of Photography*'s reviewer, however, who suggested 'in general it is perhaps better to accept the fact of their existence without inquiring into just how they arrived at their present form, because the story is a long and complicated one, and Baron Richthofen is hardly accepted as an authority today'.

In his review of the book for the *Birmingham Post*, P.R.L. Heath wrote: 'Mr Poucher, to whom the lover of beautiful scenery already owes a substantial debt, is at his best in such magnificent surroundings; his skill and experience as a writer, traveller, climber and above all, photographer

LEFT: Cimon Della Pala, Dolomites.

RIGHT: Latemar from Lago di Carezza.

combine more effectively than ever to make the Dolomites a "must" for all mountain enthusiasts.'

Poucher returned to the Celtic fringe of the British Isles for his next two picture books for Country Life; *Journey into Ireland* (1953) and *The North Western Highlands* (1954). The Ireland book was the fruit of a four-month, 6,450-mile tour of the wilder, more mountainous parts of the country, starting from the Wicklow Mountains south of Dublin and heading for the west coast and the MacGillycuddy Reeks, Connemara and Kerry and finishing with the Antrim Coast and the Mournes.

But Ethel A. Miller in the *Photographic Journal,* wished that Poucher had strayed away from the mountains to record other parts of the rich Irish heritage. 'The illustrations, although technically irreproachable, are somewhat monotonously mountainous, and appear to have been made for the information of the mountaineer rather than for the delight of the

pictorial photographer,' she wrote. 'A little light relief in the form of some records of Ireland's lovely rural and river scenery, fine architecture, and curious customs would have appealed to a larger public.'

Poucher returned to the well-proven photographic journey format for *The North Western Highlands*, which he dedicated to his fellow members of the Climbers' Club, the Fell & Rock Climbing Club, the Royal Photographic Society and members of kindred clubs.

Divided into nine sections, the photographs cover those areas of Highland Scotland to the north and west of the Great Glen, including Kintail, Applecross, Torridon and Lochinver. Poucher wrote in his introduction: '. . . until the traveller has seen Glen Shiel and the great peaks of Kintail, Glen Torridon and the wonderful mural precipices of Liathach, Loch Maree and the dominating blunt cone of Slioch and the peculiarly aloof hills to the north of Ullapool that culminate in the sharp wedge of

LEFT: Cima di Lavaredo.

RIGHT: Popena and Tre Croci from Mont Ciaso Dio.

Suilven, he can have no real conception of the splendour of this vast desolation, which is Scotland at its best and the country of the connoisseur.'

Many regard *The North Western Highlands* as one of his finest books of mountain photographs, and the reviews it attracted seem to confirm this. The *British Journal of Photography* certainly thought so, adding a word of encouragement to the increasing band of 'miniature' users: 'There is something tremendously encouraging to the average photographer in the statement that out of all the lovely photographs adorning this book, all but three and the cover picture (Suilven from Lochinver) have been taken with the camera in the hand.'

John O'London's Weekly commented: 'As a photographer of hill and mountain scenery, alert of eye for the dramatic composition of cloud masses, peaks and water reflections, for the sweeping interplay of sunlight and shadow over naked rock or the dazzle of snow, Mr Poucher is perhaps unsurpassed today.'

A different format was adopted by Country Life for Poucher's last book with them, which was to be the first in which his colour photography appeared. *Climbing with a Camera: The Lake District* was published in 1963 with a full-colour cover and identical frontispiece of the Scafells from Border End and eight colour plates inside. The back cover also featured a portrait and short biography of the photographer for the first time. Half-page pictures predominate and Poucher's text is interspersed with the images in what might be called a magazine style. There is far less technical photographic information too, as if the publishers were aiming at a more general, tourist market for the book.

The title suggests that this was to be the first of a series of *Climbing with a Camera* volumes, but in the event *The Lake District* was to be the only one to be published. This may have been because by this time Poucher's allegiance had transferred to Constable, who had already produced *The Lakeland Peaks* and *The Welsh Peaks* in the Pictorial Walking Guide series.

Interestingly for this book Poucher chose to follow almost the same route through the district he had chosen for his first book *Lakeland though the Lens* twenty-three years previously, starting from Mardale (by now completely flooded by Haweswater) but in this case finishing with the Scafell Pikes.

The title was again very well received by the reviewers, *Mountain Craft* even suggesting that it reached so high a standard of production that it was 'unique as an illustrated literary work'. No less distinguished a contemporary than C. Douglas Milner, reviewing for the *Photographic Journal*, said the book, like its many predecessors, would give considerable pleasure to hill walkers who did not practice photography. As for the photography, however, Milner had some critical comments about the advent of colour.

> Price has doubtless limited the number of . . . colour prints which could be provided, but those of us who know the district can read colour into the wide selection of fine reproductions chosen from the author's collection. Though half tone does not quite reach the best

The Scafell range from Border End.

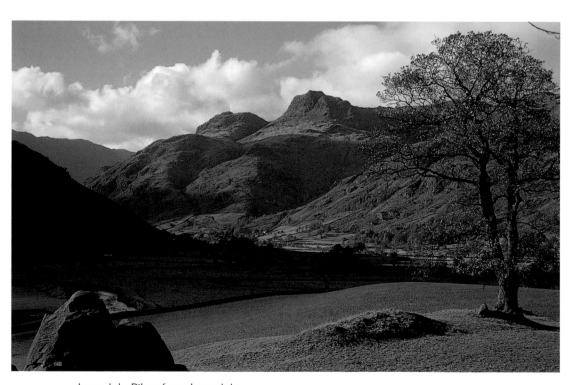

Langdale Pikes from Langdale.

A Camera in the Hills

that gravure can provide, the quality here is high and as in all the volumes produced for Mr Poucher by Country Life, illustrations are not stinted in number.

The colour prints, he claimed, were uneven in quality, some being first rate but others showing bad blues and greens. 'No doubt the original transparencies are good, and it is always safer to reproduce muted tints than clear colours, for so often this type of distortion is seen.' Milner added, with a nice nod to Poucher's predecessors: 'The author's walking powers are to be envied, and his weight-lifting capacity is of no mean order. He tells us that he now carries two M2 Leicas with a 3G in reserve, plus a number of extra lenses. The combined weight must about equal the 10 x 8 machine of George Abraham, who was, it will be recalled, the Poucher of the Nineties.'

There is no doubt that Poucher would have gained a huge sense of satisfaction from this comparison by one of his leading contemporaries to the great pioneers of Lake District mountain photography, the Abraham brothers of Keswick. But by now his thoughts were already turning to the production of practical walking guides to Britain's mountains using his photographs as the backdrop. And as fate would have it, a top London publisher was also thinking along the same lines.

6. WALK THIS WAY

I've striven on Tryfan
And trod on Y Garn,
Been lost on Siabod,
Spun many a yarn
'bout trips on the Carnedds,
Crib Goch, Lliwedd too,
You ask why I do it?
Because it's terribly good for one's character.

G.L.F., 1966

A chance find at a Stratford-upon-Avon book fair during the writing of this biography gave me the first indication that there could well be a dedicated band of 'Poucherists' out there, in addition to the collectors of all Alfred Wainwright's Lakeland summits and the obsessive Munroists north of the Border.

The book (I paid just £5 for it) was a first edition of Poucher's *Welsh Peaks* from 1962 in its original dust jacket and in pretty good condition. But that wasn't what attracted me to it (I'd already got a well-used copy myself); it was what I discovered inside. Pasted in cut-out paper strips on each route map were details of when and with whom the owner of the book – an anonymous 'G.L.F.' – had completed each carefully coloured route. That wasn't all; G.L.F. had also penned and inserted pieces of prose and humorous poetry (see above), which he had written describing his love of the hills, and a tick-off list of essential equipment (including, interestingly, pyjamas and tie) required for his expeditions.

The seventy-two summits listed at the front of the book had been assid-

Is this G.L.F. on the Cantilever Stone, Glyder Fach?

uously ticked off by G.L.F., presumably as he'd done them, and only fourteen remained to be completed. And to top it all, there was a 35mm transparency of a walker, perhaps G.L.F. himself, perched on the famous Cantilever Stone on the icy, rock-splintered summit of Glyder Fach, inserted between the musty pages.

Unfortunately, there is no way of knowing exactly who G.L.F. was, other than the fact that he was a mountain lover as the inscription in the front of the book simply says, in an apparently female hand, 'To "The Climber", Christmas, 1964'. As G.L.F. did many of the routes with his family, it would be nice to think that perhaps she came along with him on some of the trips.

Poucher had signed for the top London publisher Constable for the first of his unique pictorial guidebooks, *The Lakeland Peaks*, published in 1960 at a price of 16s (80p). Apparently it was a happy coincidence that both parties had been thinking along the same lines, so when Constable approached Poucher, he was delighted to find a new publisher for his idea.

The Lakeland Peaks (now in its twelfth edition and reissued by Frances Lincoln in 2005) was followed by *The Welsh Peaks* in 1962 (now in its eleventh edition reissued by Frances Lincoln in 2005); *The Scottish Peaks* in 1964 (ninth edition also reissued by Frances Lincoln in 2005), and finally, *The Peak & Pennines*, which was published in 1966, which ran to five Constable editions. *The Magic of Skye*, a revised reprint of Poucher's 1949 classic, was reprinted by Constable in the smaller and some would say, less appropriate *Pictorial Guide* format in 1980, running to three editions.

Poucher's great innovation, never succesfully imitated, was to mark the routes across his photographic prints in white ink, making the way ahead obvious to even the novice hill walker. He did all this annotation himself, drawing the routes and naming the peaks in his own handwriting across his black and white prints.

The first editions of the *Pictorial Guides* (a description he may, or may not, have copied from Wainwright) were supported by maps featuring the distinctive italic lettering of John Bartholomew and Son of Edinburgh. Interestingly, and probably because of crippling Ordnance Survey royalties, the latest editions of the *Pictorial Guides* published by Frances Lincoln have reverted to Bartholomew mapping, except in the case of *The Scottish Peaks*, which have new sketch maps drawn by Martin Collins.

Each handily-sized, rucksack-friendly book was produced to an identical format; between 40 and 140 routes are described ascending all the major peaks and groups in each area with effusive introductions by Poucher and brief descriptions of the routes. Readers were expected to be able to find their way by combining the routes outlined on the photographic plates, plus the maps. It was a winning combination, and the books sold in their thousands.

Each volume had its own distinctive character, however. *The Lakeland Peaks*, for example, was bound in dark blue cloth boards, *The Welsh Peaks* in green cloth covers, while the *Scottish Peaks* and *Peak and Pennines* reverted to those distinguished silver or gold lettered dark blue cloth boards. Like so many well-made books, the early Pouchers also had their own distinctive, sharply-musk *smell* too, an important feature for booklovers.

The start of each book, after Poucher's usual flowery introduction, had notes on equipment, rock climbing, the best accommodation centres for exploring the peaks and usually a table of heights of the peaks, passes, lakes or tarns. *The Welsh Peaks* and *The Scottish Peaks* also included a glossary and dictionary of common placenames in Welsh and Gaelic respectively – very useful for the *sassenach*.

The equipment sections of the early editions make interesting reading in today's world of high-tech Gore-Tex jackets, lightweight boots and walking shoes. Poucher's standard still-life photograph of the essentials always included a sturdy canvas Bukta rucksack, a length of climbing rope (hardly

WAP's size 10½ Tricouni nailed boots.

WAP, equipped for the hill, cigar in mouth and Leicas around his neck, at Crag Lough, on Hadrian's Wall.

necessary for the vast majority of his routes), and a stout, wooden-handled ice axe (ditto).

As for clothing, Poucher claimed it was perhaps a question of personal taste, 'there are many mountaineers who merely wear their oldest cast-off suits, often with brilliant patches as a decoration,' he advises. There are not many mountaineers today who would be seen dead on the hill in a cast-off suit with patches, and you are much more likely to bump into over-equipped walkers on even the gentlest of Lakeland fells wearing Everest-specification Gore-Tex jackets and boots costing many hundreds of pounds. Times and fashions change, and Poucher swore by his faithful draw-stringed anorak and plus-fours which, he said, 'allowed more freedom about the feet'.

Poucher was very particular about stockings, and recommended, as essential for the walker's comfort, thick red woollen oversocks. Why red? 'I have advocated the wearing of RED [his capitals] because it is more easily seen on the hills and in case of accident will facilitate quick discovery and location,' he explained in *The Lakeland Peaks*.

Headgear was another bone of contention, he said. 'For years I wore none at all in the hills, and then one summer day on the Napes I got a slight touch of sunstroke. . . . I first wore a soft cloth hat that would not blow off in a high wind, but have now discarded that in favour of a bobcap, which in my view is ideal for the climber.' And while we don't know what he might have thought about the now ubiquitous baseball cap, he does a bit of an about-face about caps with peaks. 'Peaked caps,' he says severely, 'do not look right and are rather frowned upon by the climbing fraternity, but so far as I can see there is very little objection to them, excepting that in rain the water runs down the back of the neck.'

In each book, he described and photographed in loving detail a different

A Camera in the Hills

type of climbing boot, starting with heavy Tricouni, clinker and mugger-nailed English-made soles in *The Lakeland Peaks*. These were followed by Swiss-made vibram-soled boots in *The Welsh Peaks* and Italian vibrams in *The Scottish Peaks*. By the time he had reached *The Peak and Pennines* in 1966, he had apparently finally succumbed to the vibram revolution, while still expressing his doubts of their effectiveness in wet and slippery conditions. 'There are advantages and disadvantages in vibrams,' he wrote. 'They are silent and easier on the feet on *dry* rock, but on *wet* rock or moss-covered slabs they can be a handicap to rapid progress because the utmost care becomes imperative to avoid a slip which in an exposed situation might result in a twisted or broken ankle.'

In each volume of the *Pictorial Guides*, Poucher also gave notes on the calculations of distances and times for the routes, some tips for route finding in mist, how to alert the emergency services and give a distress signal if in difficulties and explanations of the 'Brocken spectre' and of 'glory', when a rainbow-coloured ring appears around the climber's shadow in misty conditions. The *Peak and Pennines* also included a brief description of the route of

Cul Beag and Loch Lurgain from Stac Polly.

Coire Mhic
Fhearchair.

the 250-mile Pennine Way long-distance path, with a warm tribute to its founder, Tom Stephenson, and *The Scottish Peaks* also features the classic long walk through the heart of the Cairngorms, the 27-mile Lairig Ghru.

In *The Welsh Peaks*, published in 1962, Poucher appealed to older walkers to not be put off the ascents of the higher mountains. He described the last time he attempted the famous Snowdon Horseshoe (Pen y Pass, Crib Goch, Carnedd Ungain, Snowdon, Lliwedd) at the age of sixty-five, completing the 3,089 feet of ascent in eight 'leisurely' hours. 'Since this book will be read by men and women of all ages, these figures may be discouraging to those in advancing years, and in these circumstances, I think it will be useful, and perhaps indeed inspiring, to give the times taken over this magnificent lofty ridge. . . . So, to those of you in the sixties and seventies, I say, "Have a go!"'

As might be expected, there were always extended notes and tips on mountain photography, including Poucher's '13 essentials for good moun-

A Camera in the Hills

View of Stac Polly.

tain pictures', which featured in every volume. These ranged from the camera – and unsurprisingly Poucher plumped for the leightweight Leica as his favourite – through the types of lens, filters, film, lighting and composition.

Significantly, the modern Frances Lincoln editions of Poucher's *Lakeland, Scottish* and *Welsh Peaks* exclude the author's specific note on the now virtually universal genre of colour photography. When Poucher first wrote these books, black-and-white photography was still the order of the day, and colour was in its infancy. Interestingly though, Poucher's note on the choice of film has been retained, although in the light of the digital revolution, photographers who are still using film are fast becoming a rarity.

Poucher always had much to say about composition, and he gave examples of well-composed pictures in each volume. In *The Scottish Peaks* he even evoked the spirit of the great artists El Greco, Leonardo, Raphael and Tintoretto by describing, with an explanatory diagram, the importance of placing the subject of the picture in the Golden Section. He illustrated this

ABOVE: Snowdon from across
Llyn Llydaw.

RIGHT: Tryfan in winter.

Mam Tor from
Castleton.

with a photograph of Stac Polly (Pollaidh) and Loch Lurgainn, in which the mountain's summit occupies that crucial position giving 'a feeling of balance and order, even excitement in dramatic conditions – the interest is demanded'.

Finally, and apparently in response to readers frequently asking him what was the best view of and from certain mountains, he described in great detail what he considered to be the best place, times and conditions in which to record each mountain or range of hills to the best effect. He was later to complain that one of the biggest mistakes he made as a photographer was that he gave all his secrets away.

The photography in the *Pictorial Guides* represents some of the best of Poucher, some would say spoiled by the scratchy lines of his directional walk routes across the pictures. Among many memorable images, a few stick in the memory, such as the magnificent frontispiece to *The Scottish Peaks*, a snow-draped Liathach from Loch Clair, which extracted a typical Poucheresque caption: 'Liathach in snowy raiment'; the winter view

RIGHT: Liathach from Loch Clair

BELOW: Tryfan from Llyn Caseg-fraith

A Camera in the Hills

described in the introduction to this book across the ridges of Blencathra from Scales Fell from *The Lakeland Peaks*; his classic and frequently reproduced winter view of Snowdon from across Llyn Llydaw, and the often-repeated view of the reflected side-lit buttresses of Tryfan in the waters of Llyn Caseg-fraith in *The Welsh Peaks*.

He even managed to impart some mountain majesty to lowly Mam Tor at the head of the Hope Valley in the Peak District with another winter view taken from a barn near Castleton in *The Peak and Pennines*, which also features a dramatic *contra jour* shot of Kinder Reservoir from the lip of Kinder Downfall and a moody, misty shot of Ingleborough from above Ingleton.

One of the most unusual series of photographs Poucher took for *The Peak and Pennines* was the sequence of shots in which he recorded ascents by one of Britain's most legendary rock climbers, Joe Brown, on two of the most famous routes on the Roaches in the Staffordshire moorlands. Poucher recorded that Ken Meldrum had arranged the meeting, at a time when Brown was Chief Instructor at the Derbyshire County Council's White Hall Outdoor Pursuits Centre, on the moors above Buxton.

Banneau Sir Gaer.

Sequence showing Joe
Brown climbing on the
Roaches.

Brown told me that he had very little recollection of that day over forty years ago, but he was seconded by John Amatt, whom Poucher described in the guide as his 'pupil'. 'Of course, it was well known in climbing circles that, rather extraordinarily, he wore make-up, although I don't recall noticing that,' said Brown. 'He wasn't a climber, but his reputation as a mountain photographer at the time was quite high.'

The sequence of shots showed Brown climbing what is still one of the hardest overhang and roof climbs in Britain, the Sloth, on the Roaches Upper Tier. Graded HVS (hard very severe), the Sloth was first climbed by Don Whillans and Brown in 1954 and was so-named for the amount of time the climber spends hanging upside down like the slow-moving South American toothless mammal. This was at the time when between them, Brown and

Whillans were pushing British rock climbing to new, previously unheard of, extremes in what was known as 'the working-class revolution' in the sport.

Brown recalled that Poucher had scrambled up to the boss of gritstone to the right of the route to take the memorable sequence. They show Brown climbing up to and swinging out from and over the over-hang, with Amatt belaying him and watching anx-iously beneath. Poucher also recorded Brown and Amatt climbing the well-known hand-jamming route of Saul's Crack, also graded HVS, further along the Roaches Upper Tier, for the guide.

The books were as usual, warmly reviewed, although *Mountain Craft* complained that the photographs in the first volume on *The Lakeland Peaks* were 'not quite up to the usual high standard of the author's previous works, but we suspect this to be a fault of printing and not of photography'. It was kinder to *The Welsh Peaks* published two years later, claiming: 'Rebuffat, Terray and Greenbank (top rock climbers at the time) tell us how they do it; Poucher tells us how to get there.' *Country Life* described it as 'monumen-tally useful and inexpensive'. The price then was 18s (90p).

The late Tom Weir's rather grudging review of *The Scottish Peaks* in *Country Life* was also critical of the photography. 'In the photographic notes the author favours the miniature camera. It is certainly convenient, but I could do with sharper pictures, though the results are effective enough.' *The Sunday Times*, however, in a rare review of a guidebook, said that 'the pictures have an aesthetic as well as a functional quality. Anyone setting out for Scotland with mountains in view should take Mr Poucher's book in his pocket.'

Strangely, the book which covers perhaps the most heavily-walked areas of Britain, *The Peak and Pennines*, was the least successful in the series. Although running to five editions, it was never as popular as the other three, which are still in print.

It was, however, initially warmly received in that World Cup year of 1966. J.E.B. Wright, reviewing for *Mountain Craft*, wrote:

> If anyone doubts the beauty or the interest of the northern moors and the Backbone of England here is convincing evidence of one of the most attractive of our English heritages [*sic*]. Here is one of our greatest masters of landscape photography, and of mountain literature, giving us another example of his wide knowledge of mountains and mountaineers. The fine photographs, the precision of the map routes, the technical chapters on weather, equipment for walking and climbing, mountain photography and the hazards of mountain country all fit perfectly into yet another example of the erudition of this great mountain man.

One suspects that Poucher would have loved that, coming as it did from the pen of one of Britain's top mountaineers.

Climber claimed that Poucher's *Peaks* series had become the rucksack companions of a great many hill walkers and hill-going photographers, and *The Peak and Pennines* was 'a most welcome addition covering . . . one of the most popular hill areas in the country'.

His editor and close friend at Constable from the 1980s was Miles Huddlestone. 'We published his guides to climbing in Wales, Scotland, the Lakes, and the Peak and Pennines with marked success,' recalls Huddlestone,

Kinder (Hayfield) Reservoir from Kinder.

Boxing Glove Stones, Kinder.

Great Gable from Wasdale.

'and I was responsible for incorporating his meticulous revisions in the innumerable revised editions. He was particularly concerned that the safety of walkers and climbers would not be endangered by any mistake of his.'

Poucher was notoriously scrupulous in checking his routes, although he admits in later editions of his *Welsh Peaks* that the two variations of the route he had described in the first edition for the ascent of Y Garn II from Bwlch Gylfin 'are not yet freely accessible'. To obtain the view he got of Snowdon from the slabs on the northern face, he said, would require the permission of the local farmer. The photograph of the shorter variation, which skirts beneath the northern face, was omitted from later editions.

Someone who can vouch for Poucher's meticulous care to keep his routes revised and up-to-date is his friend John Ellis Roberts, former Head Warden for the Snowdonia National Park, a body he served for thirty-three years before being made redundant in 1999. 'I first had contact with Poucher in 1971, and from that time Walter asked me to keep him updated on changes to his routes,' explained Roberts.

Blencathra from Castlerigg.

In those days, his *Welsh Peaks* was the bible for hill walkers in Wales, so when a footpath changed due to a legal diversion, to try to overcome erosion problems, or the erection of a new footbridge, I would always let Walter know. He would then visit the site to update his photographs.

A case in point was when he had shown two routes at the start of the PYG track on Snowdon which actually joined higher up. For management reasons, I asked him to delete the lower route, which he did without question.

John Ellis Roberts continued:

I was a great fan of Poucher; he was very courteous – an absolute gentleman and I thought his photography was just wonderful. He was quite happy to share his photographic secrets with anyone, as he did in many of his books. In the days before mobile phones and GPS, we often actually used his books following accidents in the mountains, when someone came off the hill to report an accident and wasn't exactly sure where the casualty had been left. We could show them his photographs and we could usually pin it down pretty accurately.

I had a personal experience of Poucher's painstaking regard for detail in his guidebooks when I was employed in the Information Section of the Peak District National Park in the mid-1970s. In the process of revising his *Peak and Pennines* for its third edition, Poucher had sent a letter to the National Park enquiring about the origin and significance of a line of stakes crossing the peaty summit of Bleaklow. I was able to tell him that they had been erected voluntarily by pupils of Chesterfield Grammar School to mark the boundary between the parishes of Charlesworth and Hope Woodlands.

In a charming letter of appreciation, Poucher wrote back: 'I experienced very poor weather on this trip and could work only on one and a half days owing to rain or dense fog on the hills. However, next time I am your way I will give myself the pleasure of calling, because I find personal contact a most valuable asset in my work.' It was to be the closest I ever came to meeting him.

After the Constable titles were acquired by the present publisher, Frances Lincoln, in 2005, it was decided that, forty years on, the time had come for a major overhaul for the still-popular guides. Poucher's photographs in *The Lakeland Peaks*, *The Welsh Peaks* and *The Scottish Peaks* were all re-scanned from the originals and new prefaces written by Poucher's son John, who always took a proprietorial interest in his father's work. The publisher reverted to the use of Bartholomew's mapping and for the first time, the books were issued in paperback with a full colour cover, now at a price of £12.99 each. All the routes in *The Lakeland Peaks* have been thoroughly revised by Peter Little; those in *The Welsh Peaks* by mountain guide Nigel Shepherd, and in *The Scottish Peaks* by mountaineers Kevin Howett and the former editor of *Climber*, Tom Prentice. The introductory notes on equipment have been revised and updated, and antiquated features like the comparative details of climbing boots have been removed and replaced with notes and pictures of modern equipment. These include a photograph of lightweight boots and a modern Lowe Alpine day sack, and the photograph of suggested clothing now includes a peaked cap, a fleece, Gore-Tex waterproof jacket and gaiters.

But thankfully, the explanation of the Golden Section remains in *The Scottish Peaks*. *The Peak and Pennines* volume has not been re-issued because of poor sales due to increased competition from the wealth of walking guides to this ever-popular area.

Poucher's *Pictorial Guides* were groundbreakers in their day, combining top mountain photography with precise route and location details in a handy, rucksack-portable format. They were a joy to consult if you were planning a route at home, to use as practical guides on the hill, or reflecting on the past day's walking. They made Walter Poucher a household name, but he then was never shy of being recognised or picked out in a crowd, as we will discover in the next chapter.

View from Ill Bell to Thornthwaite Beacon with WAP.

7. DESCENT INTO COLOUR: THE LATER YEARS

'Can we meet somewhere later and talk,' said a breathless Elizabeth Taylor. 'I've never seen anyone look quite so marvellous in my life.' This is not, as might at first appear, a report of her first encounter with Richard Burton, Eddie Fisher nor any of her galaxy of other consorts and husbands.

No, the object of her obvious fascination was the then eighty-eight-year-old Walter Poucher, and it happened in 1980 at the Swiss ski resort of St Moritz, where they were both staying on holiday. The brief encounter was reported by Sue Arnold in her 'Upfront' column in the *Observer* magazine in September 1981.

Arnold added: 'Having met Mr Poucher myself, not, alas, in the mountains of St Moritz but rather in the foothills of Reigate, I cannot but agree with her. For a man [then] in his ninetieth year Walter Poucher is, to say the very least, astonishing.'

It was his make-up, not his camera, his climbing nor his chemistry, which had attracted Taylor 'and thousands of other women over the decades' Arnold continued. '. . . the meticulously applied cream blusher, the subtle lipstick, the five layers of jet mascara – for daytime he prefers navy blue and leaves off two layers. Mr Poucher is a living, walking testimony that good make-up expertly applied can make you look a million dollars.'

Elizabeth Taylor, of course, had a strong personal interest in cosmetics and perfumery herself. Who can forget her lavish use of mascara in her title role in the 1963 film, *Cleopatra*, the first time she worked with Richard Burton and the film that made her the highest paid actress in the world at the time. She has launched over 6,700 fragrance products under her name, including well-known perfumes such as Passion, White Diamonds and

WAP, cigar in hand, in later years at the Thornthwaite Nursing Home.

Mont Blanc from
Aiguille du Midi
cablecar.

Black Pearls, which together still earn her an estimated $200 million in annual sales. In the autumn of 2006, the by now ennobled and eight-times married Dame Elizabeth Taylor celebrated the fifteenth anniversary of her White Diamonds perfume, one of the world's top ten best selling fragrances over the past decade. The unlikely couple obviously had much in common they could talk about.

Sadly for Arnold, Poucher was not wearing any make-up when he met her in his Dolomite Sprint (his doctor had advised him to sell the Jaguar for something smaller when he was seventy-five) at Reigate station. He said it was because his wife did not care for it. 'I don't mean to brag,' he added, guiding Arnold to a window seat in the bar of the Walton Heath Golf Club, 'but when I'm done up properly for the evening with my Panstick and eyeshadow I look absolutely marvellous. Women adore it. "Walter," they used to say, "advise me

Chamonix Aiguilles at sunset.

on *my* make-up and I won't lock my bedroom door tonight."' On hearing that, Arnold said she perhaps understood why Mrs Poucher wasn't that keen.

When asked if he ever wore make-up in the mountains, he replied: 'Only Panstick – it's the best sun protection going. When I first went to Hollywood as a consultant I was using Touch and Glo, but all the movie stars (including perhaps his friend Liz Taylor) swear by Panstick and I've never used anything else.' The many walkers who met him on the hill will dispute that claim, because the mascara, blusher and lipgloss were often prominent.

Had his wearing of make-up, wondered Arnold, ever been *misunderstood*? 'If you mean do people think I'm a pansy, never,' he replied emphatically. 'Elizabeth Taylor said she wished more men took as much trouble with their appearance. Mind you,' he added with typical Poucher chutzpah, 'I do it exceptionally well.'

Monte Rosa from above summit of the Matterhorn.

Finally, as he drove Arnold back to the station, he couldn't help giving her a little advice too. Looking her carefully up and down, he said: 'Do yourself a good turn. Go and see two nice girls I know who run an outfit called Cosmetics à la Carte. They're trained chemists and they'll fix you up with your own personal kit. Modern make-up is a miracle. Without it a beautiful woman is still beautiful. With it, she's *sensational*.'

In addition to the stars of Hollywood, Poucher also consorted with Royalty, and as we have already learned, the late Queen Mother rated his perfumes as her favourites. As mentioned in Chapter 4, he once spent over an hour in the company of Queen Mary when she paid a visit to the first Norfolk lavender harvest and nearby distillery at Fring in September 1936. He had been in Norfolk conducting tests on the new crop for Yardley, and in obviously self-generated stories which appeared in his home town *Horncastle News* and *Lincolnshire Standard* newspapers later that week, he described with obvious pride his meeting with the Queen:

> I was in the company of the Queen, who was attended by two Ladies in Waiting, for over an hour, and found her a most gracious and charming lady. First of all I conducted her over the lavender plantations, in which the Queen displayed exceptional interest and expressed a hope that the plantations would be extended, so that more lavender oil could be produced in this country. The inspection of the plantations lasted over half an hour, and I then took the Queen over the adjoining distillery, where she watched the whole process, from the extraction of the oil to the finished product.
>
> Her Majesty showed a keen and practical interest in everything she saw, asking various questions about the work in the distillery, and altogether it was a most delightful experience for me to have the honour of explaining the different processes to Her Majesty.

Forty-five years later, Poucher confided to Sue Arnold in that *Observer* magazine interview that Queen Mary had once asked him, possibly on this occasion, for advice on how to disguise a slight rash on her chin. He is said to have replied: 'With the greatest respect, Your Majesty needs a dermatologist, not a beautician.'

In a feature on the collapse of Yardley which appeared in the *Independent on Sunday* in 2000, columnist Janet Street-Porter, who had recently stepped down after three years as president of the Ramblers' Association, rather ungraciously described Poucher as 'a fully paid up member of the British Academy of Potty People', but more positively as the man who had brought affordable cosmetics to working-class women.

She described the reaction of John Ellis Roberts, her climbing guide in Snowdonia, when she had asked him to relate his most embarrassing experience. 'Without a moment's hesitation he replied, "Meeting Walter Poucher for dinner". Roberts recalls that meeting himself below.

Street-Porter, who was obviously fascinated by this man, said she had tried to interest the BBC in making a film about 'the wonderful Mr Poucher', but 'The BBC being what it is, they could not decide whether the subject was "Arts" or "Countryside" – and the project remains on my "must do one day" file.' We are still waiting.'

Poucher was a regular contributor to many outdoor magazines, including the ground-breaking *Mountain Craft* which was published by the Mountaineering Association. Roger Redfern took over as editor in 1966. 'I first met Poucher, who was accompanied by his son, John, at one of the MA's London lectures in about 1960, when he gave a fantastic talk on his North American travels,' recalled Redfern. 'He was an arresting figure in camel hair overcoat and smoking a large cigar. When I took on the editorship of *Mountain Craft*, he promised me anything I needed free of charge, and thereafter let me have photographs and articles on anything I requested. He had an amazing index system, long before computerisation, and claimed to be able to locate any photograph within 30 seconds.' Redfern was invited to visit Poucher at his luxurious apartment in Reigate Heath one August day in the early 1980s.

> I walked up the drive in monsoon conditions, and when I knocked at the door, my anorak was soaked and my shoes full of water. Walt instructed his wife Dorothy to take the wet garments and dry them while we retired to his impressive office.
>
> Towards evening, I put on my dried clothing and Walt insisted on taking me to Reigate station. It was still pouring and I recall watching him sprint 200–300 yards to the garage to bring the car to the door. We drove at high speed through the deluge – through roundabouts, junctions and heavy traffic – and he never put a foot wrong, despite only having the use of only one eye.

The unfortunate incident which resulted in his restricted vision happened in February 1967, while Poucher, at the age of seventy-six, was on holiday in Zermatt. He was apparently descending the Matterhorn when he suddenly he suffered a thrombosis which deprived him of the sight in his right eye and also severely affected that of the left. As he told Ivan Rowan in a *Sunday Telegraph* interview in May 1983: 'The doctors told me "You've got the body of a man of forty".' They apparently poured cortisone into him, but couldn't save the sight in his right eye. After further treatment back on London, the sight in his left eye gradually recovered, after the doctors advised him to rest for three to six months.

Things weren't quite as bad, however, as reported in the *Colour Group Bulletin* of the *Photographic Journal* of July 1967, which ran an obituary of

The Storr from Loch Leathan.

The Quirang.

Poucher, thus enabling him to join the ranks of the distinguished band who, like Mark Twain (who had famously complained: 'The reports of my death are greatly exaggerated'), have been able to read their own obituaries.

Poucher received get-well messages from all over the world after the Matterhorn incident, from climbers, photographers and former colleagues in the cosmetics industry, and he was able to report in a letter to readers of *Climber* in July 1968: 'You will be glad to know that my left eye is now as good as it ever will be, and that I hope to start driving a car again after a winter holiday in the sunny south.'

This visual impairment did, however, affect his mobility in the mountains, as he told Ivan Rowan in that *Sunday Telegraph* interview. With only one eye it was difficult to judge the way across rough, boulder-strewn terrain, and an attempt to climb Sgurr Alisdair in the Cuillins of Skye the

A Camera in the Hills

Sgurr nan Gillean from Sligachan.

year before with three of his originally six Good Companions had ended in failure and disappointment.

'That was the last of the summer wine,' reported Rowan. 'He goes alone now, carefully reconnoitring the lower ground for vantage points, with a bar of chocolate and a flask of coffee in his rucksack; he has even hired a helicopter to give him aerial vistas of the mountains he traversed in his youth.' This was for *The Alps*, the fifth in the colour book series published by Constable in 1983.

Roger Redfern's last meeting with Poucher was when he was in his nineties and returning from a photographic trip to the Lake District. He had just acquired a new BMW car, and delighted in telling Redfern how, as he was driving down the M6 in torrential rain, he had overtaken a long line of slower vehicles and noticed that the speedometer was recording an effortless 96 miles per hour.

They met for dinner at The George Hotel in Hathersage, in Derbyshire's Hope Valley, and after the meal Redfern asked him to sign some books he'd brought along.

> Several other guests were obviously interested to watch this arresting man signing books in gold lamé gloves. He must have noticed this and said to me: 'It's no jolly good making one's face youthful with make-up and letting the side down with the sight of gnarled, claw-like hands, old boy.' He wore white gloves during the day and gold in the evening.

'WAP was a remarkable man, a perfectionist, a great friend and a huge help to someone like me,' said Redfern. 'He once said he wanted me to follow in his footsteps, especially with his *Country Life* work. But, of course, times change and with a change of editor after WAP's death, they no longer wanted the sort of topographical pieces that he and I had done for them.'

We get a rare glimpse of Poucher's politics in an exchange of letters in *Mountain Life* magazine during the summer of 1974, when the late Chris Brasher was editor. In an editorial on the subject of walkers' and climbers' relationships with shooting landowners, Brasher had stated: 'We must respect their sport if we want them to respect ours.' This had apparently upset correspondent Tom Dale from Lancaster, who complained about the denial of access and spoiling of the countryside by the hunting and shooting fraternity, claiming that they deserved the 'continuing and active contempt and hostility' of walkers and climbers.

Poucher responded that he could not allow the letter to pass without comment 'because it smells strongly of left-wing socialism which is always steeped in ENVY [his capitals]. During the past fifty years I have been climbing our homely hills and only on the most rare occasion have I encountered incidents which might come within the sphere of Tom's "contempt and hostility."'

He quoted instances on Kinder Scout, Derwent Edge, Y Garn II and in Scotland, where, he said previous inquiries or 'a couple of whiskies with the head ghillie' had always revealed the location of the next day's sport. The climber had only to respect their wishes during September and October and could wander at will for the remaining ten months of the year. But Dave Robb of Aberdeen in the next issue responded: 'If we are all allowed ourselves to be bought off by a few whiskies very little advancement can be made.'

Seeking to pour oil on troubled waters, Brasher wrote in his next editorial: 'This is a free society and what we have appealed for is some tolerance of other peoples' points of view. Landowners who still believe that their hills are their exclusive domain must be persuaded differently. Climbers who

WAP on summit of Am Basteir.

The Turtle, Brimham Rocks.

think that they have a divine right to wander over the hills *without* regard to anybody else must also be persuaded differently. Such landowners and such climbers are anti-social animals and mercifully they are both getting rarer.'

John Ellis Roberts recalls meeting Poucher for the first time, and wondering, because of his reputation, obvious wealth, big cars and foreign holidays, whether he might be 'a bit of a lineshooter'. But over the years it became apparent to Roberts that although all these things were true, Poucher was 'an aristocrat without a title'.

Shortly after his initial meeting with him, Poucher invited Roberts to dinner at The Prince of Wales Hotel in Beddgelert. 'It was an experience I shall never forget,' said Roberts (the incident he later related to Janet Street-Porter as described above).

A Camera in the Hills

I turned up in a suit, asked for him at reception and was directed to the dining room. He was already there, sitting alone at a small table with a single candle in the corner. He was wearing a dark suit with a rose in his buttonhole and a rather loud yellow tie – but his face was completely made-up with blue mascara eye shadow, powder and lipstick.

I got a few odd glances from the locals who knew me, I can tell you, as the dining room filled up.

By 1984, Poucher's failing eyesight meant that he had to be driven to the hills and get around by taxi to meet his contacts and update his guidebooks. In October that year, he was in Snowdonia staying at The Royal Oak Hotel in Betws y Coed and told Roberts that he had to travel to the Lake District as the autumn was moving on and he had to get some more shots.

'I offered to drive him to Borrowdale in my girlfriend Liz's car,' recalled Roberts. 'It was a smallish car and when he went to pick him up, he was standing outside with four large suitcases. Somehow we managed to get everything into the car and during the journey, he was very complimentary about the car's performance – despite being used to Jaguars and BMWs himself.'

Poucher was wearing make-up for the journey and apparently discussed its merits with Liz. Roberts remembered: 'He said the reason he wore the make-up was to test for any skin reactions to new products, which could not be sent out unless they were perfectly safe.'

John Ellis Roberts was such an admirer of Poucher that in the early 1980s he made representations to the British Mountaineering Council (BMC), Lord Hunt, Chris Brasher and the chief executive of Gwynedd County Council and to see if he might be nominated for a British honour. But support from the mountaineering fraternity was apparently lukewarm. 'One person did try to use his contacts,' Roberts told me, 'but he also made the comment that Poucher had twenty-five books in print at the time, and his royalty cheques were in the region of £70,000 per annum. It was as if that was a reason not to support the nomination, so sadly, nothing came of my attempt.'

Poucher would often stay at the Pen y Gwryd Hotel or Pen y Pass Youth Hostel on the Llanberis Pass, or at the Ogwen Cottage Mountaineering School, when revising his *Welsh Peaks*. The owner of Ogwen Cottage was Ron James, a former Birmingham schoolteacher who with Tony Mason and Trevor Jones, had set up the pioneering mountain school in the early 1960s. James also has very fond memories of Poucher, who stayed there at least two or three times.

'He was a tremendous fellow and a real gentleman,' he told me, 'great company and with a real twinkle in his eye. He suggested the use of make-up was a good thing after a heavy night out to counteract the adverse appearance of a hangover!

'He was also the man who persuaded me to write and publish *Rock Climbing in Wales* in 1970, and I'm sure he put in a good word for me with Miles Huddlestone at Constable. At the time there was no comprehensive climbing guidebook which covered the whole of Wales, and Ken Wilson and I collected the climbs and photographs for the book, which I'm sure would not have happened without Walter Poucher.'

James recalled going out with Poucher very early one morning from Ogwen Cottage to capture the iconic photograph of Tryfan's snow draped east face from Helyg. 'He told me he had been there twelve times before he thought the lighting conditions were exactly right. He was a brilliant photographer, for my money the best there was.'

Veteran former Peak District National Park Ranger Ian Hurst also had an encounter with Poucher in the 1970s, when he was revising his *Peak and Pennines* guidebook. It happened on the bleak, 1,600-foot summit of the Snake Pass. 'I was at the Snake Summit meeting Pennine Way walkers when I was approached by a grey-haired, elderly gentleman,' recalls Hurst. 'Nothing striking in that you might think, but he was wearing full ladies' make-up, including powder, lipstick and eye make-up, and three-quarter-length ladies' evening gloves.

Malham Cove.

'Being an impressionable young man in my late twenties, I was somewhat taken aback and very wary. He introduced himself as W.A. Poucher
and said he was revising a future edition of his book on *The Peak and
Pennines*.'

Poucher was particularly interested to know if some cast metal fence
posts were still in situ around the Rifle Range boundary at Crowden on the
route of the Pennine Way walking towards Laddow Rocks. Hurst was able to
confirm that they were still largely in place.

Some days later he received a letter addressed simply to: 'Ian Hurst,
Crowden Warden', with his telephone number. It was from Poucher thank-
ing him for his assistance. 'I think the Post Office should have been

congratulated on such a speedy delivery with such a very inadequate address,' Hurst commented.

Ken Wilson, successor to Roger Redfern as editor of the retitled *Mountain* magazine from 1968–78 and the producer of the groundbreaking *Hard Rock*, *Classic Rock* and *Big Walks* series of coffee table mountain books, has many memories of Poucher, both as a contributor and as an important figure in the mountain world.

Of course, I was familiar with his books from an early age,' he recalled. 'Our Scout Group in Birmingham was certainly fired by the mountain images in the books of Smythe and Poucher that we obtained from the local library, but it was soon the rock climbing action shots which caught the eye.

Salt Cellar, Derwent Edge.

A Camera in the Hills

I first remember meeting him in the early 1960s when, as a young climber, I hitched a lift with him in his white wall tyred Humber Super Snipe from Plas y Brenin to Pen yr Grwyd in Snowdonia. He pulled up and said: "Would you like a lift, dear boy?" He was dressed immaculately and wearing white gloves and possibly make-up, so I was suitably impressed.

Wilson later used Poucher's photographs in his first edition of *Mountain* in 1968, and as we have already learned, they had been used regularly by the editors of its predecessor, *Mountain Craft*. As a professional photographer himself, Wilson has a more pragmatic view of Poucher's claim to a place in the mountaineering photography hall of fame.

'In my view, he was never in the pantheon of great mountain photographers like Vittorio Sella, William Donkin, Ansel Adams and Elliot Porter, and he also lacked the creativity of other UK photographers like Robert Adam, John Cleare or Gerald Lacey,' he told me.

If you asked me to name a really memorable shot by Poucher, I couldn't. But having said that, he was a consummate professional, consistently reliable and competent, who produced a very commercial and consistent standard of mountain illustrations.

He was prepared to wait for days or even weeks at his hotel (usually Gleneagles or one of the other golfing hotels in Scotland) for the correct weather conditions for his photography. Few others had that luxury, and I believe he was able to do this because of the financial security that he gained from the sales of his standard works on perfume. I greatly admired his tenacity and patience, and in this respect, he was consistently professional and his range of books display this. He explained all this to me over lunch at his favourite Walton Heath Golf Club in Surrey in 1968, when I sought his help for an early *Mountain* feature.

Wilson paid tribute to Poucher as one of the great 'movers and shakers' who had introduced people to the British hills in the post-war period through his photographic and guide books. 'There can be no doubt that many thousands were inspired by his photographic books and lectures to visit the hills for the first time.'

Poucher had been elected as associate of the Royal Photographic Society (RPS) as early as 1941, and became a Fellow in 1942. In 1975, he was awarded the highest honour in the photographic field: an Honorary Fellowship of the RPS.

Ken Wilson was present when the BMC paid tribute to Poucher at its annual dinner in Llanberis in 1983. President Tom Price presented Poucher with an engraved glass from Dentdale, describing Poucher as 'a perfectionist; a musician, a doctor of medicine [*sic*], a chemist, author, mountaineer and photographer, but above all a raconteur of tremendous interest.' At the

High Cup Nick.

age of ninety-two, Poucher had driven himself to the event from his Thornthwaite nursing home in the northern Lake District.

Walt Unsworth, then the editor of *Climber and Rambler* and owner of Cicerone Press, was a fellow Cumbrian resident, and was also at the dinner. He recalled that as Poucher said he wasn't sure of the route, he had suggested that he followed him. 'Soon after reaching the motorway we noticed he had drawn up on the hard shoulder and, thinking he might be in trouble, I stopped and ran back to see what the problem was. He said he had been 'caught short' but it was OK because he said he always carried a special bottle with him. When he set off again, he shot past us and was soon completely out of sight.

'He had told me, with a glint in his eyes, that his doctor had advised him to change his car from a very powerful Jaguar. He had – but he had exchanged it for an equally powerful one.'

WAP overlooking Crag Lough, Hadrian's Wall.

Another great admirer of Poucher was my good friend Tom Waghorn, formerly Chief Sub-editor for the *Manchester Evening News*, and a fellow member with Poucher of the Climbers' Club. Waghorn described Poucher as 'the man who turned mountain photography into an art', and recalled how he had once had to introduce him to a lecture audience in the Library Theatre, Manchester. 'The place was packed and he received a tremendous ovation,' said Waghorn.

'He emanated perfume and I had the impression that his face appeared to be made up – though I can't remember whether it was with eye shadow, mascara or blusher. Plucking up courage after the lecture, I popped the inevitable but embarrassing question: why? "Tom," he replied, looking at me gravely, "it's up to every man to make the best of his appearance."'

Waghorn, ever the professional journalist, also asked Poucher what he thought was the secret of his success. He replied rather curtly: 'Nobody else has the time nor the talent.' In his glowing obituary to Poucher in the *Climbers' Club Journal* of 1988, Waghorn described him as a supreme perfectionist', and repeated that rather vainglorious self-assessment of the man.

He would sometimes wait days for the optimum conditions for a single shot. Even in his nineties he was prepared to travel in a helicopter for the first time to take aerial pictures of the Alps for his colour book on the subject. There were, of course, other master lensmen to challenge Poucher – Douglas Milner, Alfred Gregory and Basil Goodfellow, for instance. But Poucher had that vital commercial streak and used to tell his publishers there was nobody else with the talent, the time and the money to cover the country.

Nowadays (dare I say it?) Poucher's work seems rather flat and old-fashioned compared with modern American greats such as Galen Rowell.

Another distinguished outdoor writer who met Poucher under slightly different circumstances was Paddy Dillon, who at the time was working as

Grasmoor from
Loweswater Church.

a waiter at the Wastwater Hotel (the name later reverted to The Wasdale Head Inn), in Wasdale in the western Lakes.

'I heard that Poucher was staying at the hotel on the Friday night of the August Bank Holiday weekend in 1978,' recalls Dillon.

A couple of guys at the bar were chatting about this "old poofter wearing make-up," so I knew it was him.

I was tidying up the car park in front of the hotel the following day and Poucher was out there, taking pictures of Great Gable. To me, it looked wonderfully clear and you could see every detail on the fell, but Poucher wasn't impressed. I guess he'd seen it in much better

Mickleden.

conditions over the previous decades. I don't think he climbed the fells over the weekend. Old age had caught up with him (he was eighty-seven at the time), and he just wandered round on the level.

Later, Dillon was waiting on tables in the hotel dining room, where a table for one person was less than a yard square – at a pinch they would use it as a table for two. Poucher had less than a square yard, but that wasn't enough for him, and he ordered Dillon to remove 'that silly lamp and that flower', so off went the globe candle lantern and the flower vase, and for good measure, the melba toast basket too.

'His make-up was quite thickly applied, and to be honest, it didn't look good on a man of his advanced years,' he recalled. 'He gave me his meal order,

A Camera in the Hills

then when I brought his meal, he told me to wait while he scraped the little side-salad on to a side plate and told me to get rid of this. Evidently, he was a meat, potatoes and two veg man – not at all impressed with little add-ons.

'I thought he was a bit gruff, but I was quite willing to forgive him because I'd long admired his photographs of the mountains.'

A decade later Poucher was dead, and Dillon's career as an outdoor writer was well under way. Shortly after Poucher's death, he reviewed a posthumous collection of his photographs for *Country Walking* magazine. He told me it was nice to be able to start the review with the words: 'Over a decade ago my path crossed Walter Poucher's at Wasdale Head. It was a glorious August Bank Holiday weekend and I reckoned the colours and views were superb. Not so Poucher, who took photographs but was far from impressed. I had met a true perfectionist in the field of mountain photography.'

Chris Bonington, Britain's best-known mountaineer and another Lake District aficionado, described the 'inspiration' that Poucher's books had given him during his formative years.

I first became aware of the mountains on our doorstep when I saw a book of his pictures of the Scottish hills in a friend's house in Wallasey, when I was fifteen. I was inspired.

When I started learning to take better pictures, there weren't many other mountain photographers around, and the fact that his pictures were of British hills somehow made them more relevant. Poucher's were some of the most important books around, and I was particularly grateful for the help given by the sections on photographic techniques in the hills.

Poucher broke new ground in his time, and brought to the public the beauty of our mountains through his photographic books. He didn't have the genius of Ansel Adams or some of the other great landscape photographers, but he was an excellent craftsman and has an important place in the development of mountain landscape photography in this country.'

All the photographs in the Constable pictorial guide series had been reproduced in black-and-white, but when Japanese four-colour printing became cheaper, the publishers decided that the time had come to publish Poucher's vast library of colour photographs in large-format, coffee-table editions. Many people felt that those latter colour picture books produced by Constable were not Poucher's best work, and that he would be best remembered as a fine black-and-white photographer. There are, for example, instances of Poucher's shadow appearing in the foreground of some shots – something he would surely not have countenanced in his prime – and Constable's design at times left something to be desired, as in the case of the Matterhorn summit hidden in the centre of a double-page spread in his view from Riffelalp in *The Alps*.

The titles of the large format colour books were, in order of publication: *Scotland* (1980), *Wales* (1981), *The Lake District* (1982), *The Highlands of Scotland* (1983), *The Alps* (1983), *The Yorkshire Dales and the Peak District* (1984), *The West Country* (1984), *Lakeland Fells* (1985), *Skye* (1985), *Ireland* (1986), *The Magic of the Highlands* (1987), *Lakeland Panorama* (1989), *Snowdonia* (1990) and *Peak and Pennine Country* (1991). The last book which Poucher put together himself, with help from a Constable editor due to his failing eyesight, was *Ireland* in 1986. After his death, Constable asked John Poucher if he would continue the series and he agreed, compiling the last three books, *Lakeland Panorama*, *Snowdonia* and *Peak and Pennine Country*, himself.

Of these, only *The Alps* really broke new ground, and involved, as Poucher explains in his preface, the use of cablecars to reach the Aiguille du Midi, Kandersteg and Stechelberg, and the hiring of a helicopter to get some truly spectacular aerial shots looking down on summits such as the Matterhorn. He also recounts that to achieve the unique shot looking down on the summit and Zermatt ridge of the Matterhorn, with Monte Rose in the distance, the pilot had to take the helicopter to well over 5,000 metres (16,500 feet). Perhaps he could be forgiven for using such artificial aids to get his last photographs – he was, after all, ninety-two years old at the time.

However, with uncharacteristic humility he had the grace to admit the toll of his advancing years in his preface: 'It is a good thing for athletic youth to measure its strength against these great mountains, and for elderly climbers, mountain-walkers and scramblers to know their limitations.' At last, it seemed as though Poucher was acknowledging the frailties brought on by his considerable age.

Miles Huddlestone, his editor at Constable for many years, recalled how they had selected the images for the new series from Poucher's vast library of colour photographs: 'With the curtains drawn, he and I would seclude ourselves in the study of his Reigate flat and in an enjoyable, two-hour slide-show, selected the photographs for the ensuing volumes. He would then drive me to the Walton Heath Golf Club where we would have lunch.'

He recalled an embarrassing but by now commonplace incident which took place on a sales and publicity visit to Edinburgh with Huddlestone shortly after the publication of the first full-colour volume covering *Scotland* and the guidebook format reprint of *The Magic of Skye* in 1980. Huddlestone explained:

> When away from home, because his wife Dorothy abhorred the practice, Walter would wear make-up – he was, after all, Yardley's chief perfumier and had been described rather disparagingly in some climbing circles as 'a perfume salesman who wears his wares'. At breakfast he descended the stairs to the restaurant in a pale grey suit, gold lamé gloves to hand and with powder and lipstick generously applied. The stares of the assembled hotel guests lingered questioningly over the pair of us: The Master and his Catamite? Despite the maquillage, nobody could be described as less effeminate than W.A. Poucher.

Constable's then managing director Ben Glazebrook told me he hardly knew Poucher, 'but I always knew when he'd been in the office because of the lingering smell of perfume'.

A journalist who interviewed Poucher at the Edinburgh hotel during that promotional tour was Jim Crumley, now a distinguished Scottish nature writer but in 1980, a feature writer on the *Edinburgh Evening News*. Crumley's article, headed 'Face to face with the grand old man of the mountains' appeared on 25 October 1980 when Poucher was eighty-nine.

'I'll never forget my meeting with Poucher,' Crumley told me.

> I was a bit overawed, meeting this legendary figure who in the field of mountain photography was reckoned to the best in the business, and a man who had witnessed most of the twentieth century. I remember being astounded at his appearance, because he was not exactly what you might expect for a man of the mountains. He was in a pin-striped suit and full make-up, including lipstick and mascara. I was used to fairly rugged outdoor characters like Tom Weir and Bill Murray, and Poucher was certainly different.
>
> But once I got over the initial shock of his appearance, I found him to be quite gracious and a real gentleman. I think the word which summed him up best was that one: graceful. He soon put me at my ease because he was very easy to talk to and also very interested in what I was doing.

Poucher explained to Crumley how he categorised mountains in every area by noting the best standpoints from which to photograph them in every season and at different times of the day. 'He was obviously meticulous in his planning and this was only possible because he had the luxury of time to wait for the perfect conditions to turn up.'

'There was only one thing for which I can never forgive him,' added Crumley. 'His insistence on wearing red walking socks meant that every aspiring hill walker followed his lead for years to come.'

Interestingly, Crumley discovered that Poucher had his own rather jaundiced view of his publisher's decision to reproduce his colour photographs in picture book format. 'He was dismissive of them, and I got the strong impression that he preferred to work in black-and-white.' He told Crumley that he favourite book was *The Magic of Skye*, an opinion which was apparently shared by another great Scottish writer on the outdoors, Seton Gordon. 'It was the quality of light on the island which captivated him, as it has many others.' What he thought of Constable's decision to reduce his masterwork to a guidebook format is not recorded but can easily be imagined.

Constable's board of directors celebrated Poucher's ninetieth birthday in 1981 with a lunch in the boardroom, a large book-lined study which doubled as MD Ben Glazebrook's office. Richard Tomkins, Constable's Production Director, remembers: 'Ben made a witty speech in which he recounted the sales success of *Scotland* in the previous year, and also that BCA (Book Club Associates) had done well with it. But a year later, on offer-

Ben Nevis from Corpach.

ing *Wales* to them, they turned it down. Ben then wrote to Christine Pevitt, BCA's chief buyer, in faux-Welsh which he read out at the lunch: "Look you, Christine . . ." and signed it "Ben the Book". It had the desired effect and BCA later came up with a substantial order.

Poucher was utterly unmoved, as Tomkins recalled. 'Ben could have been reading a lesson from the Old Testament. Poucher was a truly extraordinary man, but one thing he didn't have was a sense of humour.'

With the author by then in his ninety-sixth year, the photographs for *The Magic of the Highlands*, published in 1987, were selected, arranged and captioned by agreement with Poucher and the publisher by a team from *The Great Outdoors* magazine, comprising former editors Roger Smith and Peter Evans, and the present editor of *TGO* Cameron McNeish.

Thereafter, Poucher's son John did the selections and captioning for the colour books, which included two posthumous *Best of . . .* books on *Poucher's Scotland* (1996) and his last book, appropriately *Poucher's Lakeland*, which was published the following year. David Hughes, in a review which appeared in *Book Choice* and which was used on these last two titles claimed: 'He has elevated photography beyond the casual frozen moment to the heights of myth.'

John Poucher confided to Tom Waghorn that a couple of the photographs in the Lakeland volume were actually his own. 'Dad always seemed to take his pictures from the same spots,' he told Waghorn. 'Many of his 10,000 slides are similar though with different lighting, and not a lot were taken in winter conditions. When I showed him my efforts, he used to say "You're learning boy."'

But there was one other book which Poucher dearly wanted to publish but which never saw the light of day. There is an undated and uncompleted manuscript for another book, planned to be illustrated by 200 black-and-white photographs, which was to be entitled *This Delectable Land: A Pictorial Guide to Britain's Most Beautiful Mountain Scenery*. It was to cover the whole country from Devon, Cornwall and Surrey to Wales and the Lake District, with a section on rock climbing.

WAP at a Cumbrian book-signing with distinguished Lakeland photographer Geoffrey Berry (centre) and fellow Constable guidebook author Chris Wright (right). (Picture: Chris Wright)

'I do not know if this project had even been discussed with Constable, but in any case, it never came to fruition,' said John. 'I can only surmise that when colour books became a reality, my father decided to abandon it.'

Poucher spent his last years as a resident in the Woodend Country House at Thornthwaite on the shores of Bassenthwaite Lake, where, as he reached the end of his long life, his memory faded. In a letter to Roger Redfern in August 1985, his wife Dorothy wrote: 'Walter can only talk of his books and photography – his mind is vacant. He is much more frail and there is no hope of recovery. He is so well taken care of and spoilt – but it's all very sad. I have come to live up here with him, but I do not think it altogether a wise thing to have done.'

Poucher died on 5 August 1988 in his ninety-seventh year and was cremated at Carlisle Crematorium. Walt Unsworth attended the funeral at Carlisle and remembers being saddened that there were so few people there. Among them were his son John, his publisher Ben Glazebrook, and his old friend from Snowdonia, John Ellis Roberts, who had travelled up for the ceremony. In accordance with his wishes, his ashes were later scattered along

Arkle from Loch Stack.

A Camera in the Hills

with those of his second wife Dorothy, who had died just three months earlier, by John and Tony and his wife Joan on the green slopes of Low Fell, which overlooks Loweswater and Crummock Water in one of the quietest reaches of the western Lakes.

The legendary Alfred Wainwright, author of the idiosyncratic best-selling series of *Pictorial Guides to the Lakeland Fells*, wrote to John Poucher on hearing of his father's death: 'He has been a hero of mine since his *Lakeland Through the Lens* (his first book in 1940) was published. He was a perfectionist with the camera and I greatly admired all his work in the last fifty years. I met him only once as he was returning from three weeks in Scotland when he had never taken a single picture because conditions were never right.

'His great love, as mine is, was the Lake District. He will be greatly missed. He had a wonderful innings and I am sure he enjoyed all of it, but a future without a new Poucher is a bleak prospect for me and countless others.'

After his death, John Poucher and his wife felt that his friends would like to see him remembered in some way, so they presented memorial seats to the Woodend Country House at Thornthwaite; the Sligachan Hotel on the Isle of Skye, the island which he loved dearly, and the National Mountaineering Centre at Plas y Brenin, Capel Curig in Snowdonia, an area where he had spent many happy times. When the Woodend Country House became a private residence, John Poucher found the seat was missing, so he presented an identical one to the Scafell Hotel in Rosthwaite, the owner of which his father had known for many years.

Each seat carries a plaque bearing the following simple but eloquent inscription:

IN MEMORY OF
WALTER POUCHER 1891–1988
A RENOWNED MOUNTAIN PHOTOGRAPHER
WHO LOVED THE WILD PLACES

FACTS AND FIGURES

Poucher wrote forty-one original books, of which there were thirty-three editions, twenty-eight reprints of originals and nine reprints of editions.

Total number of copies printed:

      Large format black and white: 81,000

      Guide format: 333,790

      Colour books: 358,190

      Total: 772,980

Total number of original photographs used:

      Black and white: 3,293

      Colour: 1,397

Copies of photographs published:

      Black and white: 86,073,120

      Colour: 35,613,320

INDEX

ACKNOWLEDGMENTS

First and foremost, I owe an enormous debt of gratitude to Poucher's only son John, who lent his unstinting support to the project right from its outset but who died at the age of eighty-seven during the book's preparation, and so unfortunately will never see the result. When a question needed to be asked, John was always there with a courteous, helpful answer. He also made me very welcome on my visits to his Cumbrian home, lent me his father's voluminous scrapbooks, and not least made freely available the large number of images in his father's library which grace this book. His son Tony (Poucher's grandson) of Chichester, Sussex, who provided the carefully-annotated Poucher family album, also lent his support and with his wife Joan was also of immense assistance.

Robert Calkin, a former young colleague of Poucher's at Yardley, was very helpful on the years of his life spent in the perfumery industry, as was Bernard Nicholson, former managing director of the company. In the publishing world, Ben Glazebrook and Miles Huddlestone, both formerly of Constable Publishing, were helpful with their memories of their star author.

And I am very grateful to many friends from the outdoor world, including Chris Bonington, Joe Brown, Jim Crumley, Paddy Dillon, Henry Folkard, Ian Hurst, Ron James, Harvey Lloyd, Rennie McOwan, John Manning, Jim Perrin, Roger Redfern, John Ellis Roberts, Ronald Turnbull, Walt Unsworth, Tom Waghorn and Ken Wilson for sharing their memories of the great man or for giving me useful leads. Especially warm thanks are due to my old chum John Cleare, bon vivant and partner in several books and memorable adventures in the hills both at home and abroad (a worthy photographic successor to Poucher himself), for his honest and perceptive foreword.

Matt Brosnan, Documentation Officer in the Department of Art at the Imperial War Museum was very helpful in tracing the John Singer Sergeant and J. Hodgson Lobley pictures of the 41st CCS, where Poucher had served during the First World War.

Finally, Grant and Val Jarvis of Jarvis Books of Froggatt, Derbyshire were, as usual, a mine of information about the world of mountaineering literature, and have supplied me with many out-of-print Poucher titles over the years.

Roly Smith, Bakewell, 2007